LIE BACK AND THINK OF BRITAIN

BILL SHIPTON

WESTBRIDGE

First published in 1988
and reprinted in 1991 by
Westbridge Publishing Ltd
260 Pentonville Road
London N1 9JY

Printed and bound in Great Britain by
BPCC Hazell Books, Aylesbury, Bucks.

ABOUT THE AUTHOR

Bill Shipton is 33 years old and a regular columnist for *Penthouse* and *Club International*, an occasional feature writer for *Fiesta*, and editor of the *Daily Girls* series. His ambition is to have a job he can tell his Mum about.

INTRODUCTION

"'Ere, Bill, have you heard the one about...?"

I don't know how many miles a year I do finding out about intellectually challenging subjects like mud wrestling, but it's enough to know that the British Rail chicken and mayonnaise sandwich is the only one worth having. During this time, I find myself in a number of public drinking emporia – well, you know how it is, one has to be sociable, and generally by eleven, I'm sociable as a newt! It's there and then that people start telling me jokes.

I can't walk into a pub without hearing about another man walking into a pub with hilarious and usually bawdy consequences. If I happen to mention that I'm working for *Penthouse* or some similar serious publication, the flow increases. The trouble is, people always expect me to respond and I never remember the jokes. So when the time comes for my turn... silence, followed by desperate alcoholic gibbering.

"There was an Englishman, no, he was Scots or was it Irish, and he went into a bar, no, he was in the bar, and hang on..."

Then somebody suggested writing them down. It worked! I had a constant supply of stories at my fingertips. And now, so do you!

I've put them into the same categories I have at home, based on when and where I heard them. I'm not saying a joke 'belongs' to a particular place, but it's just where I happened to be at the time.

The only snag is, now you know them all, what am I going to tell in the pub? Perhaps if I dash out for a quick one or two, somebody will tell me some more. Cheers!

ACKNOWLEDGEMENTS

This is the page that only gets looked at on very long train journeys after reading everything else including the copyright details and the bar code.

So did you enjoy it?

Oh!

Just like the Oscars, nobody seems able to start a book without thanking all those who helped produce it. However, in this case nobody has! I did it all myself in the spare bedroom!

But if you'll excuse the indulgence, this seems as good a time as any to be nice to a few people you won't have heard of. It's cheaper than sending Christmas cards, and believe me if you ever met any of them, you'd like them too.

So my heartfelt gratitude to Sue in Birmingham (and sometimes Bromsgrove) for the wine, Alex for the beer and my neighbours Sue and John for the salt (and other things I keep forgetting to buy). And thanks too to Suzy the floozy for allowing me more time to finish the book by persistently standing me up!

Most of all, thanks to Lyn for her patience, kindness, concern and Walnut Whips. I don't know why she's so good to somebody like me, but I owe her a lot (a pot of tea, a slice of chocolate cake and numerous stamps at the last count).

THIS MIGHT SEEM A WASTE OF A PAGE, BUT WAIT UNTIL YOU FIND YOURSELF IN A BRITISH RAIL TOILET WITHOUT ANY PAPER....

LONDON
AND THE
SOUTH EAST

Ah, the South East, home of Yuppies, Dinkies and millions of Wallies. Like hundreds of others I did as Norman Tebbit suggested and came down here on my bike looking for work. It was stolen. By now, it's probably part of a surrealist statue on the South Bank called Aphrodite and the Raleigh Dawn Cruiser.

When I got here I found everyone is designer mad. They wear the labels of their clothes on the outside, so I did the same. Why anyone should want to know I'm a 36 waist, hot wash, cool iron, is beyond me.

They say that Southerners are unfriendly, and won't talk to strangers. Nonsense! Just ask one how much his house has gone up in the last five years and you won't be able to stop him talking! When they ask "How are you doing?", they generally mean on the Stock Market. And their humour...judge for yourself.

A lighthouse keeper called Crighton
Married a young lady from Brighton.
But ships ran aground
And trawler men drowned
Cos she refused to be screwed with the light on.

James and Fiona decided to go for a long walk in the summer sunshine along the Thames. They were very much in love, and meandered along the towpath for hours hand in hand. Then suddenly, James noticed Fiona was looking a bit tense.

"What's the matter, Fiona?" he asked.

"Well, I didn't like to mention it before, Jimbo, but I desperately need a pee."

"Oh dear, look we can't do anything about it now, there are people around. Perhaps if we walk a bit further we'll come to a quiet stretch."

However, the further they walked, the busier the river became.

"Jimmy, darling, if I don't go soon, I'll-"

"Hang on, old girl, not just now, there are people picnicking."

So they walked a bit further. Five minutes later they still hadn't found a secluded area.

"I'm sorry, Jimmers, I'm just going to have to -"

"But where?"

"I'll do it over that footbridge. People will think we're just sitting talking."

"Oh all right, Fi, if you must."

With that, Fiona walked on to the bridge, positioned herself over the water and slipped down her knickers.

"No, Fiona, not now!" warned her lover. "There's a punt coming."

Fiona looked down.

"Don't be silly, Jim-Jams! That's just a reflection."

Wentworth's members found it quite droll
When one played a round with Miss Cole.
He let his hands slip
As he showed her the grip,
Then four strokes later he sank in the hole.

The student nurses were taking their exams at St Thomas's Hospital, and were doing the final viva voce test before being allowed on the wards.

"Student Nurse Green," asked the examiner. "How do you tell an oral thermometer from a rectal thermometer in the dark?"

The nurse thought hard.

"I know," she said. "Taste it."

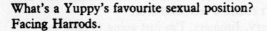

What's a Yuppy's favourite sexual position?
Facing Harrods.

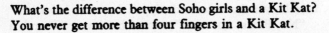

What's the difference between Soho girls and a Kit Kat?
You never get more than four fingers in a Kit Kat.

Two pilots at Heathrow were having a debate about the merits of different types of aircraft.

"In my opinion, you'd have to go a long way to beat the old Trident," said one, a fresh-faced youngster.

"Rubbish!" replied his colleague, a pilot of the old school. "None of the jet planes had the character of the older prop ones. Take the Britannia – now that's what I call an aircraft!"

"The Britannia!" exclaimed the younger man. "Turbo prop planes are hopeless. They're impossible to handle. Now the Trident had three jet engines..."

"And the Britannia had four propellers," interrupted the old pilot. "And I know which I'd rather handle. Four screws beat three blow jobs any day."

In Camden, a libber, styled Ms,
Cried out when she needed a ps,
'Ladies and gents,
Are terms I'm against,
I'm a person. I shall go where I pls.'

What do you call a Sloane Ranger on a water bed?
Lake Placid.

The boss and his secretary were out for a meal together. After a lengthy but delicious dinner, the bill arrived. The boss picked it up.

"I insist we go dutch," said the secretary immediately. "You pay for the food and the wine and the rest of the evening will be on me."

Reginald, a top executive with his company, had tried every diet he could think of to lose weight. He'd started on the Beverly Hills, moved on to the Cambridge and ended with the High Fibre, all to no avail. Now his doctor had told him he had to lose weight or he was in danger of suffering a stress-related heart attack.

"You know your trouble," said his wife one night, deciding a blow to his pride might be the answer. "You've got no will power. You're always sneaking off for snacks."

Reginald was not used to being talked to in this way.

"What do you mean, no will power?" he shouted.

"You haven't. Look at John Jackson down the road. Now he's got will power. He's given up smoking and drinking, and never looked back."

Reginald's pride was mortally wounded.

"Right," he said. "You want to see will power, I'll show you will power. From now on, I'm sleeping in the spare room."

With that he stormed out of the bedroom and made up a single bed in the small guest room. This wasn't exactly what his wife had had in mind, and nobody was more surprised than her when he stayed there the next night and the night after, and so on for three weeks. To tell the truth she was extremely miserable.

On the twenty-second night of their separation, Reginald was settling down in the small bed when he heard a timid knock on the door.

"Yes, what is it?" demanded Reginald self-importantly.

"It's only me, dear," said his wife.

"Well, what do you want?" he asked sternly.

"Can I come in?"

"I suppose so," he said, still trying to sound officious.

When she did, the sight that met his eyes was one he hadn't seen for a long time. His wife was wearing a short see-through nightie with black stockings and nothing else. Her hair was brushed and his favourite perfume issued from the dark tempting recesses of her body. She sauntered over and sat on the bed next to him. Then she ran her hands down her breasts in the way he had before their little argument.

"Y-y-yes, w-w-what is it?" he said trying but failing to sound as if he was still totally in control of his emotions.

"I just wanted to tell you..." she said running her fingers through his hair "...John Jackson has started smoking again."

Yuppies say that sex is like an American Express card. You should never leave home without it.

How do Sloane Rangers talk to their babies?
"Gucci, Gucci, goo!"

Henry and his Sloane Ranger girlfriend Sarah had been 'walking out' for some time.

"I say, Sarah old thing," said Henry one night. "I don't want to be a bore and all that but don't you think it's time we did it?"

Sarah burst into hysterical giggling.

"Don't be silly, Henry," she said slapping him playfully. "Never before marriage, don't you know.

Might get Harry Preggers. That would be simply awful. Tell you what though, I'll sort of do it with my hand. I'll get my gloves."

Henry decided to settle for that, but as she started work, he began to gasp, go purple and his head bobbed up and down violently.

"I say, Henry old fruit, you get jolly excited don't you what?" she said.

"Not always, Sarah," he replied. "It's just you've got your bracelet caught in my Old Etonian tie."

What's a Sloane Ranger's idea of a perfect sexual relationship?
Simultaneous headaches.

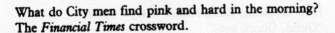

What do City men find pink and hard in the morning?
The *Financial Times* crossword.

In the Eastbourne hotel, two elderly ladies sat reminiscing in the lounge. Suddenly the Palm Court Trio started playing some febrile dance music.

"Oh Ethel," wittered one. "I loved dancing. Do you remember the minuet?"

Her deaf friend looked up.

"Good grief, of course not," she replied. "These days I can hardly remember the men I screwed."

In matters penile and testicular,
Surrey girls are highly particular.
Their great predilection
Is for an erection
That maintains a precise perpendicular.

Basildon Barry was a bit of a wide boy who liked souped up cars and lager. It was a Saturday night and once again he had been down the disco and pulled a young girl. Then he drove her back to his place in his Cortina with the go-faster stripes, plied her with Malibu and lured her into bed. He started to strip for action.

As he undid his Top Man Hawaiian shirt, Tracey, the girl of that particular moment, noticed a tattoo of a rose on his chest.

"'Ere what's that then?" she asked.

"Oh, the tattoo?" said Barry. "I had a girl called Rose once, and she was really hot, know what I mean, so I decided to have a tattoo of a rose to remember her by."

"Oh I see," said Tracey, a bit miffed.

Then Barry undid his C&A Avanti trousers to reveal another tattoo, this time of an ivy leaf.

"'Ere, you've got another one," commented the half pissed but perceptive Tracey.

"Oh, the ivy leaf," said Barry totally unconcerned. "That was for a girl called Ivy who was just the best kisser in Essex, know what I mean?"

"Yeah..." said Tracey, more than a little disconcerted by now.

Then Barry whipped down his extra brief acrylic underpants to reveal yet another tattoo on the end of what he would describe to his mates as his 'love truncheon'.

"Blimey, what's that a tattoo of?" demanded Tracey as it wobbled towards her.

"It's the British Telecom symbol," replied Barry with a smirk.

"Oh yeah?" said Tracey suspiciously, "and which girl's that for?"

Barry grinned and leaped on the bed.

"It's for yoo-hoo!"

Graffiti spotted in the gents toilet of a pub in Covent Garden.

"I'm ten inches long and three inches wide. Are you interested?"

And written underneath in different handwriting...

"Amazed! But what size is your willy?"

Albert had always promised his wife a shopping expedition to the West End, and finally got around to arranging it. However, as soon as she was preoccupied by the windows in Regent Street, he took the opportunity to disappear for a jaunt around Soho.

Almost as soon as he reached the back streets, he approached a young prostitute.

"How much for half an hour with you?" he asked eagerly.

"Ten pounds," came the reply.

"Oh dear, I've only got £2.50. That's all my wife let's me have."

"I'm sorry, darling," smiled the young lady, "but you won't get much for £2.50 around here."

Albert tried again, but always met with the same answer. So he decided to spend his money in a nearby pub instead. But just as he was sipping his first pint, his furious wife walked in.

"Albert! I might have known I'd find you in a public house," she shouted. "Still, since we're here you can buy me a drink."

Meekly, Albert went to the bar, got the drinks and sat down to hear a torrent of abuse interrupted only by stories of bargains she'd taken advantage of in the shops. He was just hearing how she had snapped up a dress for only £250 when one of the prostitutes he'd accosted walked in. He blushed.

"Hello there," said the tight-skirted floozy, sitting down next to him.

"Er hello," he replied shyly.

Then she spotted Albert's wife.

"There, what did I tell you?" she grinned. "I said you won't get much for £2.50 around here."

At the Oxford Street temp agency, a young girl was filling out a form for office work. She was blonde and buxom but not well stacked with 'O' levels. About a third of the way down the form, she came to a question which asked simply, 'Sex M or F?' She thought long and hard.

The agency manageress looked at her.

"Do you have a problem?" she asked.

"It's this sex M or F question," she replied.

"Really?" said the manageress somewhat surprised. "Don't you understand what the initials mean?"

Suddenly, the young girl's eyes lit up.

"Oh I get it now," she said happily. The manageress looked relieved. "It's obvious, I'm an F," she continued. "I haven't masturbated since I was fourteen!"

What do Camden health food fanatics call pubic hair?
Organic dental floss.

Overheard at a Sussex bridge club.
"I think sex is a bit like bridge. If you've got a good hand, who needs a partner?"

How do you separate the men from the boys in Covent Garden?
With a crow bar.

After ten years of happy marriage at Guildford barracks, Sgt Wendy Buller took her husband Capt Frederick Buller to the divorce court.

"Now tell us, Sergeant, in your own words, why you are seeking a divorce from your husband?"

"It's our sex life," she wailed. "It's disastrous."

"Forgive me interrupting," said the magistrate, "but

you have three lovely children. It can't be that bad."

"That was before Freddy did his SAS training," sobbed the young wife.

"But the SAS are renowned for their fitness and stamina," he continued. "I would have thought that should have improved his sexual performance if anything."

"Oh the SAS made him fit enough, I grant you," wept Wendy. "Trouble is, they also trained him to get in and out of sticky situations without anyone noticing."

A young actor went to his doctor handily placed next to the West End theatre where he was appearing.

"Doctor," he said, "I have this strange rash near my genitals. Shall I strip off?"

The doctor, an ex-Thesbian himself, boomed.

"Only, my boy, if the part warrants it."

Lecherous manager Marvin Box spotted a buxom blonde in the bar of his small out-of-town theatre. Sidling up to her, he tried his usual line of approach.

"You know, you could have a real future in the theatre. Have you ever thought of becoming an actress?"

The blonde stopped drinking her gin and tonic, but continued chewing her gum.

"You really think I could be a stage star?" she said in a broad Cockney accent.

"I certainly do," replied Marvin. "Why, you're already starting to make it big!"

Recently a survey was carried out on the subject of newspapers read by commuters on the train. The results were as follows:

The *Times* is read by people who run the country.

The *Mirror* is read by people who think they run the country.

The *Guardian* is read by people who think they ought to run the country.

The *Daily Mail* is read by the wives of people who run the country.

The *Financial Times* is read by people who own the country.

The *Daily Express* is read by people who think the country should be run as it used to be.

The *Daily Telegraph* is read by people who think it still

And the *Sun* is read by people who don't care who runs the country, so long as she's got big tits.

History tells us that London's first sperm bank was an unmitigated disaster. There were only two potential donors. One missed the tube and the other came on the bus.

Jim the station master at Waterloo took British Rail's 'Customer Care' policy a little too literally, and decided to entertain a lady commuter from the 5.57pm in his flat. He hadn't received a caution signal all evening, so they wound up in bed. As his heavy goods was about to enter her tunnel, she suddenly noticed with alarm that he wasn't wearing a condom.

"Oh Jim, darling, do be careful. I'm not on the pill, you know," she whispered.

"That's alright, madam," he replied. "At British Rail we always pull out on time."

Following the success of CAMRA, the Campaign for Real Ale, in London, a group of men and women in Battersea, fed up with oral sex, are launching a Campaign for Real Sex. It's called CAMSHAFT.

A lady from the City called Basset
Was understandably tacit,
When her legs did the splits
Skiing in St Moritz,
And she froze her principal asset.

Two golfers were sitting in the club house of their Surrey golf course discussing the relative merits of local links.

"You know Uffington Manor's just got a lady pro?" said one of the oldest swingers in town.

"Really? What's she like?"

"Beautiful. Blonde, slim with a lovely little bottom."

"I must get down there."

"Wouldn't bother if I was you," grumbled the old man. "Smithers says he deliberately got into the rough with her last week."

"And..."

"He declared her an unpliable lay."

A new gay club has opened in Hammersmith where men gather to play the latest card game, Pooftah Poker. The rules are the same as for ordinary poker except that all the queens are wild and straights don't count.

There's a barrister girl we admire
Who fills the High Court with desire.
To our intents and beliefs,
She never bothers with briefs,
No wonder the judge wants to try her.

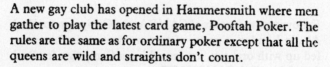

Two executives, determined to keep fit, were working out in an exclusive West End gym.

"I say, Johnson," said one, "I hear you're going out with that girl who comes to the mixed class on Thursday."

"That's right," he replied.

"What's she like?"

"Fabulous," said Johnson. "She's amazingly fit. She takes her exercise very seriously. She believes in concentrating on building firm muscles one at a time."

"Really?" said his colleague. "And which particular muscle is she working on at the moment?"

The executive smiled.

"Mine!"

Lady Lawdown was breakfasting at the Savoy and making a big fuss about her order.

"Now young man," she demanded of the waiter, "make sure the toast is crisp, I'd like the egg soft but not runny, and I will not abide sausage with the mixed grill. One sight of sausage makes the short curly hairs on the back of my head stand on end."

"That's a coincidence," said the cheeky waiter. "One sight of short curly hairs makes my sausage stand on end!"

Two promiscuous female drama students sat in their Clapham flat.

"How did you get on with that new bloke last night?" asked one of the flatmates.

"Terrible!" replied the other furiously. "Talk about selfish…"

"How do you mean?"

"He insisted on using one of those condoms with the little lumps on to increase the sensation," Sally moaned.

"That doesn't sound so bad to me," commented her friend.

"You're joking!" exploded Sally. "He wore it inside out."

Cynthia, a beautiful young deb, was now 18 and about to leave for the hunt ball with her new boyfriend, Piers. She was dressed in the finest outfit her London designers could produce, and she looked every inch the young lady of wealth that she was. Her only problem was her naivety. She had led a very sheltered existence in Hampstead, and so her Mummy thought it was time to give her some advice.

"Now before you go, I'd like to warn you about a couple of things, Cynthia," she said.

"Oooh weeely, Mummy, do you have to?"

"Yes, I do. Now at this party, I dare say you will be dancing cheek to cheek with this Piers friend of yours. Mummy won't worry about that. You may even have a few drinks with him. Mummy won't worry about that either. He may then take you back to the car, kiss you and start to put his hands inside the front of your dress. Mummy wouldn't be too worried about that. But if by any chance he tries to get on top of you, then Mummy would very definitely start to worry. Do you understand?"

"Oh yes, Mummy," replied Cynthia.

Despite this, Cynthia didn't return from the ball until half past four in the morning. She almost fell in the door. Her hair was awry, her designer dress torn with wine stains down the front, and her stockings were almost in shreds. Her father was furious.

"Really, young lady, what time do you call this?" he demanded. "Whatever happened? Your mother has been worried sick."

"Oh, Daddy darling, I don't see why, I did everything she told me," she sighed. "Piers and I danced cheek to cheek, knowing Mummy wouldn't worry about that. Then we had a few drinks, and I knew Mummy wouldn't worry about that either. Then we drove off in his car. We stopped, and he started to kiss me and put his hands inside my dress, and I let him because Mummy told me she wouldn't be even worried about that. Then he took my pants off..."

"Good grief, child," cried the old man. "Whatever did you do then?"

"Oh it's okay. He didn't climb on top of me."

"Thank God!"

"No. I got on top of him, and thought, let his Mummy worry."

Two old theatrical agents were sitting in a theatre bar discussing old times.

"Eh Lou," said the first. "Do you remember when I used to manage the Ivy Benson Band?"

"I do, Emmanuel," replied his colleague. "Now look, you couldn't manage one of them."

In a pub in Brixton, two West Indians were having a piss when they were joined by another dark-skinned gentleman. The two West Indians watched as he syphoned his python, then one whispered to the other in amazement.

"Hey, man, did you see that? Dat guy was black with a white penis!"

"No, Winston, you're wrong dere. He's a honky, but he works as a chimney sweep."

"Then how come his tool is snow white?"

"He goes home for lunch."

Two jealous rival old ladies met for tea in a quaint Sussex tea shoppe.

"You know my daughter Jemima is doing ever so well for herself now," said one. "She has a beautiful penthouse flat in the West End, lots of expensive clothes, men just dying to go out with her all the time, and a new sports car for her business."

"Really! What a coincidence!" replied her friend. "My neighbour's daughter is a hooker too."

After a long day at the office, George rolled off his wife having made another perfunctory attempt at sex.

"You make no effort to satisfy me," nagged his wife.

"Yes, I do," protested George. "But I need encouragement. Why don't you tell me when you're having an orgasm?"

"Because, darling," she sneered, "you're never here."

A plush new hospital wing was being opened in Surrey by the lady Health Minister. She was invited to meet all the patients who were staying there except one who was completely surrounded by screens.

"What's behind the screens?" she asked.

"Oh, that's the vasectomy case. It must be time for his tests," replied the doctor accompanying her.

Before they could stop her, the Minister had parted the screens and gone inside. There was a man frantically playing with himself.

"Ahem," said the doctor. "It's a routine post-op test. He has to do that once an hour to check the tubes aren't leaking."

"Oh I see," replied the lady MP and, though surprised, continued on her rounds. A little later, she came to a ward where another bed was surrounded by screens. Again before anyone had a chance to stop her, she pulled them apart to reveal a young nurse on top of the patient, enthusiastically giving him lip service of the most pleasant kind.

"And what, may I ask, is going on here?" she demanded.

"Oh, er, it's another post-operative vasectomy test," replied the doctor quickly,

"You said that about the other man," she replied tetchily. "If that's the case, why is this young lady involved?"

"As you so often say yourself," replied the doctor quickly, "there are advantages in going private."

Did you hear about the young Soho dancer who took her driving test?

She failed because when she stalled the car at a junction, out of habit she climbed into the back seat.

THE SOUTH WEST

Ooooh ahhh! It's down to the land of clotted cream and the cream of clots. Yes, the South West – home of the village idiot! Of course, it isn't really like that. Just because every farm hand I know has a car sticker saying 'Young farmers do it in wellies' is no reason to think they're all stupid.

In fact, a lot of those living in the South West are shy and retired – retired stockbrokers, retired bankers, retired managing directors...But who can blame them? The countryside is magnificent, and there's nothing more relaxing than watching the farmer's crops change with the seasons. Golden with barley in autumn, rich brown earth in the winter, green and pleasant in the spring, and then covered with caravans in the summer.

Seriously, I have strong family connections with the South West and go there whenever I can. Besides, the beer's cheaper than London.

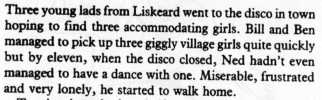

Three young lads from Liskeard went to the disco in town hoping to find three accommodating girls. Bill and Ben managed to pick up three giggly village girls quite quickly but by eleven, when the disco closed, Ned hadn't even managed to have a dance with one. Miserable, frustrated and very lonely, he started to walk home.

Turning into the lane half a mile from his house, he happened to notice a field of newly ripe pumpkins. The moon was shining on their smooth surfaces, emphasising their rounded curves, and to a terminally frustrated and slightly inebriated Ned, they looked like the body of a beautiful naked girl waiting in the field just for him. He stood admiring the sight for a few seconds until he swore he could hear her crying out for him. He got more and more excited at the thought until he could stand it no longer. He rushed into the field.

As he reached the pumpkins he lay down amongst them, running his hands over them as if they were the firm breasts of the girl he longed for. Then he grabbed two more and squeezed them in his hand, like the buttocks of the strong country lass he so desperately sought. This made him feel even more worked up, so he decided to go the whole hog. Grabbing his knife, he cut a hole in a fifth pumpkin, and started to make love to it, crying out the first female name that came to mind.

"Oh Susie, Susie," he moaned as he thrust into the vegetable. "I love you so much."

Ned was just about to satisfy his pent-up emotion when suddenly he felt a hand on his shoulder.

"Good evening, sir, and what might we be doing?"

It was George the local policeman.

"Unless I'm mistaken you seem to be molesting a pumpkin, sir," he continued.

"Pumpkin?" replied Ned, thinking as fast as he could. "My God, it must be midnight already."

HMS Libido was moored at Plymouth awaiting a tour of duty in the Med, and being refitted especially. To celebrate the old crate's refurbishment, a high ranking lady officer had been invited to inspect the ship and its crew. Come the day of the inspection, the crew lined up and piped her aboard, but instead of the old battle-axe they'd all expected, the officer turned out to be a very attractive woman in a tight fitting uniform. In fact, as she passed along the row, one able seaman found himself getting rather excited and his bellbottoms began expanding alarmingly. When the officer reached the seaman, she looked down at the inflamed area.

"What is your name, Able Seaman?" she demanded.

"Wilkinson, ma'am, Able Seaman Wilkinson."

"And what do you call that bulge in your trousers?"

"I suppose, ma'am," he said lamely, "you could say it's a one-gun salute!"

Esmerelda and Ermintrude from Yetminster were walking along Weymouth pier when they were accosted by a seaside photographer. Quickly he whipped out his camera and started adjusting the aperture.

"Oh Esmerelda, let's wait a minute. I think he wants to focus," said Ermintrude.

"Oooh really," she replied. "What both of us?"

Despite being brought up in a tiny Dorset village, Melissa had always wanted to be an actress. After years of applying for everything in *The Stage* she finally landed a role and was told to go to London to start rehearsals. When she got there, however, she found it was a show featuring live sex. In her first scene, she would be required to dress in a schoolgirl's uniform, strip it off and dance naked on the stage. Then the male lead would come on and make love to her. However, it was a show, in the West End, and good money, so she wasn't going to turn it down. There was one problem she was dreading though: explaining it to her

Mum who was not used to sinful city ways. Finally after her first night, she could put it off no longer.

"It's a musical, Mum, and I've got the most important part. I really get to show off my assets. Everybody will notice me," she said. "In fact, you'd be amazed at the people who turned up to see my opening."

"That's nice, dear," replied Mum. "Do you have a big role?"

"Oh yes! I play a young girl who's constantly put upon. Things get on top of her, and though I don't say much, I have to get very emotional near the climax."

"That sounds very good," said her Mum, obviously impressed. "And did many people come?"

"They certainly did, and they were most appreciative," replied Melissa. "By the end, there wasn't a dry hankie in the house."

As his wife lay in bed, Old Farmer Piles from the Somerset village of Ryme Intrinsica searched everywhere for a clean pair of socks.

"They're in the third drawer down on the left as usual," said his wife irritably.

However, in his haste for hosiery, the old man opened the third drawer on the right instead. He found no socks but the sight that did meet his eyes totally baffled him. The drawer was empty save for three fresh peas and £15 in cash.

"Darling?" he asked, forgetting his urgent need for socks, "Whatever are these peas doing here?"

His wife blushed, and then started sobbing.

"I'm sorry, Arthur, I must tell you the truth. Over the years I haven't been totally faithful to you. And every time

I've been with another man I've put a pea in that drawer to remind me of how naughty I've been," she replied frankly.

Arthur was at first shocked by his wife's confession, then quite touched by her openness and how upset she seemed. Three affairs in twenty years of marriage wasn't bad, he thought. Putting his arms around her, he decided it was time he too was honest.

"Don't upset yourself, love," he whispered. "I too have had my lapses. Don't let's get upset about it."

Then he remembered what he had been looking for, and his wife's instructions, more carefully. He opened the correct drawer, and sure enough, there were his socks. Pulling them on, he smiled at his wife, thinking what a wonderfully patient woman she was.

"Oh, by the way, that £15 in the drawer. Is that yours too?" he asked.

"Yes, aren't I lucky?" his wife replied, her face brightening. "Last week peas reached £5 a bushel, so I went out and sold my collection."

An elderly farmer from deepest Somerset went to the doctor's and explained that though he was in his sixties, he'd rather like to perk up his sex life a little.

"Well, I can give you some tablets, Farmer Jones," the doctor replied, "but I must warn you, they are pretty strong."

The farmer took the jar of pills with him but, distrusting drugs at the best of times, when he got home he decided it might not be a bad idea to try them out on his livestock first. So carefully he mixed a couple with his prize bull's feed. The bull ate a little of the cowcake, and the farmer watched in amazement as the pills took effect. Within the space of fifteen minutes, the bull mated with all thirty of his cows, and then tried to repeat the process until the farmer penned him safely in an adjacent field. This scared the farmer so much he decided to throw the pills away, and without thinking, he tossed them into the old well outside his house.

A few days later, the doctor met the farmer in Yeovil market.

"Ah Farmer Jones, I'm glad I've caught you," he said. "Those pills I've given you. I've just had a letter from the drugs company to say that they're too concentrated for human use. You didn't take any did you?"

"No, I didn't," replied the farmer.

"Thank God for that. In that case, can you let me have them back?"

"I'm afraid not. You see, I threw them down my old well."

"Oh no," said the doctor, somewhat alarmed. "What if somebody drinks the water?"

"Chance would be a fine thing," said the farmer. "We haven't been able to get the handle down for five days."

Did you hear about the OAP who streaked at the village flower show?
He won first prize for his dried arrangement.

What do you call farm hands with an IQ of 180?
Somerset.

A paranoid Lothario from Poole
Discovered red spots on his tool.
Cried his doctor, a cynic,
"Get out of my clinic!
And wipe off that lipstick, you fool."

A young Bristol hooker called Hurst
In the pleasures of men is well versed.
Reads a sign overhead
As you lie on the bed,
'The customer always comes first.'

Two Dorset men were sitting in the pub discussing what they'd received for Christmas. After the usual round of socks, caps and ties, one suddenly piped up.

"And I got one of they virgin detector kits."

"Whaaat?"

"A virgin detector kit," he repeated.

"What's he be like, then?"

"Well, you get a tin of red paint, a tin of green paint, a tin of blue paint and a mallet?"

"Oh yeah? Then what do you do?"

"You paint your parts with red, blue and green stripes, and show it to the girl who claims she's a virgin."

"And?"

"Well, if she says, 'Blimey I've never seen one with stripes before!' you hit her with the mallet."

Standing outside the tiny cinema in their nearest town, two young Cornish girls watched as the bill poster changed the hoardings.

"Oooh look," said one. "*Rambo*'s coming!"

The bill poster looked down at her.

"No, love," he grinned. "That's just the paste off my brush."

There's a Torquay lady called Maud
Who's renowned as a bit of a fraud.
In company, we're told,
She's frigid and cold,
But get her alone – oh my Gawd!

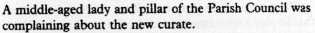

A middle-aged lady and pillar of the Parish Council was complaining about the new curate.

"He's so young, and always making eyes at all the girls," she told everyone in the village pub.

"And that's not all..." said one rather more glamorous lady from the corner. "He tried to get me into bed the other night."

"My God!" cried the Parish Councillor, "Whatever happened?"

"He trapped me in the village hall doorway," recalled the girl, "and started pulling my knickers down. Then he began singing."

"Good grief, what did he sing?"

"Cleft of ages, rock for me."

Albert was a typical hen-pecked husband. He'd moved to Taunton with his wife because she told him that they needed to be near her mother, and he hated it. There was nothing wrong with the place – he was just bored. His wife hated him doing anything, especially going to the pub and playing darts, so most of the time he had to stay at home and watch the television with her.

Then one evening, he managed to sneak out while she was asleep. He had intended to go to the pub for a quick game of arrows but as he walked down the road a car drew up beside him. Inside was a sumptuous blonde dressed as a schoolgirl. She beckoned for him to get inside.

"Come with me," she said. "I want you to make madly passionate love with me."

"But I haven't any money," he said.

"That's okay, I'm not a prostitute. I'm a bored housewife. I've seen you in the pub, and I can see you're as bored as I am. So I thought I'd get you back to my place for a few naughty love games."

"Oh!" said Albert, pleasantly surprised.

When they got back to her place, the blonde insisted that he play a schoolmaster and she the naughty girl. He'd write things on a slate and if she got them wrong, he'd have to pull her panties down and give her a spank on the bottom. Then, slowly she stripped in front of him, letting him caress her naked body before they fell into bed for a long session. By half past ten they were both exhausted, and the girl bid farewell to Albert.

"See you again soon," she said. "Oh, and why not take this piece of chalk as a souvenir?"

Albert put the chalk in the top pocket of his jacket.

When he got home, his wife was wide awake.

"And where have you been?" she demanded angrily.

"You know Mrs Jameson from up the road, love? Well,

she dragged me into her car, and took me back to her place. She dressed up as a schoolgirl and made me spank her bare bottom every time she got a question I asked her wrong. Then she stripped off in front of me and let me make love to her four times in a row."

His wife tapped her foot impatiently. Then spotted the stick of chalk in his top pocket.

"You liar," she said, waving the chalk triumphantly. "You've been down that pub playing darts again, haven't you?"

A young Dorset farm hand named Rollo
Remarked as he larked in the hollow,
"Darling, my dong
Is over 12 inches long."
Said his girl, "That's a hard one to swallow!"

A sergeant-major was taking his troops on a route march around Salisbury Plain, and after many miles they eventually wound up in the town centre. Standing on the corner of one of the back streets was a young prostitute. Despite exhaustion, the NCO sidled up to her.

"Excuse me," he asked, making sure he was out of the soldiers' earshot. "But how much is it for the pleasure of my company?"

The prostitute looked him up and down.

"£25," she replied.

"That's very reasonable," said the sergeant-major. "Company, right turn!"

An old gentleman got on to the last bus back from Yeovil after a night in the pub. As ever he had taken his little terrier, Scrap, with him for company. As the bus made its way through the villages, suddenly Scrap leapt off and disappeared into the bushes. The conductor rang the bell for the bus to move on.

"'Ere, hang on a minute," said the old man. "Can you wait for my dog?"

"I suppose so," replied the conductor. "How long is he likely to be?"

"I don't know," said the old man. "It all depends on whether he's jumped off for a piss or pissed off for a jump."

The vicar of a small parish in Avon had always fancied one of the lady parishioners. Every time he read the lesson, she smiled up at him from the front pew, and he smiled back. They were destined to get together at some time, and sure enough a few days later they agreed to meet in the park. It wasn't long before their relationship went from spiritual to physical and the couple fell onto the grass and started making love excitedly. At that point the vicar was stunned to hear a familiar voice.

"Good afternoon, Reverend."

"Oh! Good afternoon, Mr Banks," panted the vicar as he looked up to see one of his regulars driving past in an extremely rusty Ford Anglia. "Er, I didn't know you had a car. Very nice."

"It's my mother's but I'm glad you like it," said Mr Banks. "'Cos I'm trying to sell it. Would you like to buy it?"

"Well, no, actually, I don't need a car," stammered the vicar.

"That's a shame, 'cos in that case I shall be forced to tell the papers what I've just seen you doing with Miss Dunwoody."

The vicar was stumped.

"Oh okay then," he said. "How much do you want?"

"£1,500."

"£1,500 for that!" exclaimed the randy Rev, then he remembered the motorist's threat. "Okay, I'll write you a cheque..."

A week later the vicar was heard swearing as he tried to start the ancient and expensive Anglia. At that point, Mrs Wells, one of the parish's snootier residents, walked past.

"Oh really, vicar, whose ghastly old banger is that?"

"It's mine," replied the vicar.

"Yours!" said Mrs Wells. "Who gave you that then?"

"Nobody. I bought it."

"You bought that!" she continued. "You paid good money for it?"

"£1,500 to be precise," said the vicar resentfully.

"£1,500?" replied Mrs Wells. "Really, Reverend, somebody must have seen you coming."

Lady Beatrice lived in a huge stately home in Wiltshire with her two pet dachshunds for company. The two animals, a dog and a bitch, were well known locally, and so a journalist from the local paper was sent to interview her about them.

"Tell me, Lady Beatrice, have you ever thought of mating the two dogs?" he asked.

"Good heavens no," she replied, absolutely horrified at

the suggestion. "I wouldn't dream of letting Fifi be tampered with in that way."

"But what do you do when she's on heat?"

"Oh that's simple, I put her in a special bedroom prepared just for her on the top floor where naughty, naughty Marmaduke can't get at her."

"But what's to stop Marmaduke going upstairs when you're not looking?" the journalist asked.

"You silly boy. Clearly you don't know anything about dogs," Lady Beatrice replied. "Have you ever seen a dachshund manage to climb the stairs with a hard-on?"

We know a young waitress from Bude
Who's randy, raucous and rude.
She lies on the table
Till the boss cries out, 'Mabel!
That money's to pay for the food!'

A young farm hand was recently married to the village beauty queen, and after toiling for hours in the field was looking forward to getting his own oats. Eventually he finished work, threw off his jacket, ran into the house and grabbed his new wife.

"Come upstairs, my darling," he bellowed, "I want to make love to you until the cows come home."

"I'm sorry, my darling," she replied sorrowfully. "I can't, you see. I've got my woman's monthly."

"So what?" shouted the farm hand. "I've got the *Farmer's Weekly*, but I ain't planning to read it now."

Despite being the proud owner of a 300 acre farm, Arthur had never managed to even get close to the attractive milkmaid he'd employed last year. Then one day it was too much. He stood next to her watching his prize bull servicing one of his herd of Jersey cows.

"Oh, Belinda," he whispered. "You don't know how much I'd give to be doing what that bull is doing right now."

The milkmaid looked non-plussed.

"Well why don't you?" she said. "It's your cow."

There was a young lady of Exeter
So sexy that men craned their necks at her.
One man was so brave
He decided to wave
The distinguishing marks of his sex at her.

Mark and Philippa's wedding had been frantic from the start and by the end of the reception, they only just made it on to the train to their honeymoon in Torquay. Leaping over the barrier, they opened the door, just as the train was pulling out of the station and hauled themselves inside. They sat down in an empty compartment completely flustered as the ticket collector arrived.

"Only just made it, then?" said the West Country BR man.

"Yes, that's right," panted the new groom.

"Can I see your tickets then, please?"

"Of course," he replied. He reached into his pocket and handed him a scrap of paper.

"Oh dear, sir," said the dour West Countryman. "You've got the wrong ticket there. This is a special one entitling you to a lifetime's free rides but it's not valid on the 3.45 to Penzance."

"Really?" said the bridegroom panicking all over again.

"That's right, sir. It's your marriage certificate."

Two Devon girls who had been brought up at the local convent went to the disco in Barnstable. Jennifer had enjoyed herself a great deal but her more religious friend Rosemary was not so keen. As they walked home, two local lads spotted them and started chatting them up, then grabbing them. Rosemary immediately appealed to the Lord for help.

"Forgive them, God, for they know not what they do!" she cried.

"Be quiet, Rosemary," snapped Jennifer. "Mine does."

Three kids from small unprofitable small-holdings were sitting by the river discussing how much they'd like to be wealthy and the best way to achieve it.

"If I could," said the first bedraggled urchin, "I'd like to be covered all over in gold. Then whenever I wanted anything, I'd just break a bit off."

"I'd like to be covered all over with platinum," commented the second. "That's worth even more. What about you, Billy?"

"I'd like to be covered all over with hair," replied the third boy after some thought.

"Hair. Whatever for?"

"Well, I've got a cousin in Plymouth and she's only got a tiny patch of it – and you should see the money she makes!"

Weaving down a Somerset lane in her car after a night with the young farmers in the local pub, Betsy was stopped by a policeman.

"Excuse me, Miss," said the officer. "You've been driving rather erratically. I'm afraid I'm gonna have to ask you to accompany me to the station."

"Oh dear," said Betsy forlornly.

"Unless you're prepared to do something else instead..."

With that the policeman started to unzip his flies.

"Okay, officer, if I must," she said wearily. "But that's the third of those new fangled breathalysers you've given me this week."

"Help me, help me," came the plaintive voice from the beach at Bournemouth. Alan looked around, and saw an attractive brunette buried up to her head in sand. The tide was approaching fast, and she was in danger of being drowned. Alan rushed to help her.

"Quick, quick, dig me out," she begged. "The tide's coming in all the time."

Suddenly a lecherous thought overcame Alan.

"And what's in it for me if I do?" he asked with a wicked grin.

The girl pursed her lips.

"Sand," she said.

Jeremy was walking around Bath looking in the antique shop windows when he saw a desk that he thought would look particularly fine in his study. Strolling into the shop, he asked how much it was.

"I'm sorry, sir," said the shop owner, "but I'm not prepared to sell that desk. You see it has magical properties."

"Don't be ridiculous," scoffed Jeremy. "I'll give you £500 for it."

"No, sir, like I say it's magical. I'll prove it."

With that the antique dealer patted the desk and whispered into the ink well.

"Magic desk, magic desk," he said. "Tell me, how much money have I got in my pocket?"

Jeremy tutted but then watched amazed as the desk drawer started to open and shut five times. The shop owner then emptied his pockets to reveal he had precisely five pound coins on him.

"Oh come now, you can't expect me to believe that," said Jeremy. "You could easily have set that up. Get it to tell me how much money I have in my wallet."

"Okay, sir," said the proprietor. "Magic desk, magic desk, how much money does this gentleman have in his wallet?"

The drawer started moving again, this time a total of nine times. Jeremy looked in his wallet and found to his surprise that he had a fiver and four pound coins with him.

"Er yes," he said, somewhat shocked. "But it still could have been a trick. You could have seen me get my wallet out earlier. I know. Ask it how much money my wife has in her purse."

"Of course, sir," said the antique dealer. "Magic desk, magic desk, how much money does this man's wife have in her purse at this precise moment?"

Jeremy then stood aghast as the drawer started moving in and out, in and out seemingly for ever. It finally stopped at a total of 510.

£510!" exclaimed Jeremy. "It's certainly way off the mark there. She doesn't work and I only give her £20 a week housekeeping. How could she possibly get that sort of money?"

At that moment there was an almighty crash as the desk drawers fell down and its legs flew apart.

Graffiti spotted in a pub in Lyme Regis:
"Living here in winter is like being a pubic hair on a toilet seat. It doesn't take long to get pissed off."

THE MIDLANDS

Meanwhile in the Midlands...I lived in Birmingham for seven years. It was meant to be ten, but I got time off for good behaviour. However, I still have a soft spot for Brummies. Trouble is, none has ever fallen in.

I'm being unfair, like everyone else in the country. Southerners make jokes about the Midlands; so do Northerners. Fortunately, Brummies can take a joke. They must be able to – they've had to live with some architect's warped sense of humour for the last 25 years.

But let's not forget the good points about the place. The canals, for example, are a haven for wildlife. Foxes, badgers, weasels – it's amazing what floats past. Then, of course, there's the East Midlands, famous for...er...being to the East of the West Midlands. Seriously, the Midlands are 'alroight'!

Bill, a thickie brickie from Coventry, was chosen for *The Prize is Great*, a new game show, and to everyone's surprise got through to the final round.

"Now, Bill, you've done really well so far, and now it's time for the Big Prize question," gushed the host. "Just answer this and you could be going on a Caribbean cruise including hot and cold running women for two weeks with a Ford Fiesta XR3i waiting for you when you get home and £2,000 in spending money."

"Great," said Bill.

"Now, I want you to think very hard about this one, and don't reply until you're sure you have an answer. You'll have 30 seconds but the first answer you give me is the only one I can accept. Do you understand?"

"Er yeah, Bob,"

"Okay, Bill, your Big Prize question is...how many seconds in a year?"

Bill thought long and hard as the big studio clock ticked away. Sweat poured off his brow. Finally the gong went.

"Now, Bill, do you have an answer?"

"Yes, Bob."

"So, Bill, for the holiday, the car and the cash, how many seconds in a year?"

"Twelve, Bob."

The game show host was flabbergasted.

"Twelve?" he repeated incredulously.

"Yeah, that's right," said Bill. "There's the second of January, the second of February..."

Jeff was born and bred in Wolverhampton and had one lifelong ambition – to marry a 'true' blonde. After years of going with peroxide girls from all over the Black Country, he finally found one he believed fitted the bill. So after only knowing her a few weeks, they married.

Some months later, Jeff was about to make love to his wife for the third time that night when he looked down and noticed his wife's downstairs hair was black.

"Hey, Pauline, you always told me you were a true blonde," he shouted angrily.

"Urrrm, I am," lied his wife.

"Then how come yours is going dark, our kid?"

"Well," stammered Pauline, desperate to come up with an excuse to calm him down. "You know what happens when you hit your thumb with a hammer?"

"Yeah?" replied Jeff dubiously.

"It goes black, right? Well, let's face it, Jeff, in the last six months, you haven't half given it some hammer..."

A letcherous vicar in Leicester
Had Mrs Hughes on the pews just to teicester.
He kissed and careicester,
Undressed and poceicester
And then, as an afterthought, bleicester!

"I wouldn't say that new secretary from Balsall Heath is promiscuous," said the manager of a small engineering firm. "But I went to a party at her house the other day, and she must be the only girl with her own Durex machine in the toilet."

A policeman from Nottingham Junction
Whose organ had long ceased to function
Deceived his good wife
For the rest of her life
By cleverly using his truncheon.

The engaged couple sat in the car on Cannock Chase in the moonlight. Soon they were in a long embrace and Austin had his hand up Shaz's skirt, fingering her knickers as their tongues wrestled.

"Oooh Austin, Austin, that's right," she moaned in his ear. "Now go on and kiss me where it smells."

So he drove her to Tipton.

Beryl and Eddie from West Bromwich went on holiday to Spain, and stayed in a cheap but cheerful hotel. Unfortunately, the walls being paper-thin, every sound from the next bedroom could be heard perfectly.

One night, as they lay in bed, they heard a girl screaming and pounding the bed rhythmically. Beryl sat up, her curlers flashing in the half-light.

"Ooooh, Eddie, it sounds like the girl in the next room is having a fit."

Eddie smiled wistfully.

"Yes, dear," he replied, remembering the good old days when he induced noises like that in his wife. "And a bloody tight one at that."

"Ah Maid Marian," cried Robin Hood to his lady. "Let us away to Sherwood Forest, fair damson."

"Damson!" exclaimed Maid Marian. "You mean damsel. A damson is something in a jam."

"We haven't been to Sherwood Forest yet..."

The Brummy Brothers were an unsuccessful song and dance act from Rowley Regis. They were stars of the Aston Hippodrome in their day, but had fallen on hard times. Every day they went to their agent in Birmingham city centre to see if he had any work, and every day they would get the same negative response. Then one day their trudge up Corporation Street was rewarded.

"Hey, lads," said their agent joyfully – but somewhat

inaccurately as the brothers were both in their fifties. "I've got a date for you."

The Brummy Brothers were amazed.

"That's fantastic!" cried the older of the two. "What is it?"

"Well, it's only one night..." said the agent more quietly.

"That's all right."

"...And it's in Leeds."

"We don't mind travelling."

"...And it's only £10 between you."

"Oh!" said the Brummy Brothers in chorus. "Never mind, we'll do it."

However, when they got home, the brothers realised that for that sort of money, they wouldn't be able to afford to travel up there. They thought about hitching but decided it was impossible. Then one read in the *Evening Mail* of a narrow boat company taking loads to Leeds which gave free lifts to passengers who were prepared to help open locks. The Brothers rang immediately, and booked a boat travelling north the next day.

When they got there, however, they discovered the nature of the cargo they'd be travelling with. It was dung from the local farms going to Leeds to be turned into organic fertilizer. Still, it was too late to change their minds, and the ride was free, so the song and dance act climbed aboard and they set off.

As they approached the first lock, the lock keeper lent out of his cottage window, and shouted to the boat owner.

"Hey, what are you carrying?"

"Ten tons of dung and the Brummy Brothers," he replied.

At the next flight, the same happened again.

"What are you carrying?" asked the lock keeper.

"Ten tons of dung and the Brummy Brothers," replied

the boatman.

In fact the same happened at every flight between Birmingham and the outskirts of Leeds. Then after five days they approached the city, by the Leeds/Liverpool canal, with just two flights of locks to go.

"What are you carrying?" asked the last but one lock keeper.

"Ten tons of dung and the Brummy Brothers," shouted the boat owner, then felt a tug at his sleeve. It was Joe Brummy, the older of the two ageing artistes.

"Excuse me," he asked quietly.

"Yeah, what is it?" said the gruff boatman.

"We're nearly in Leeds now, and there's only one flight of locks to go."

"Yeah, so?"

"I just wondered," asked the old man meekly. "Do you think we could have top billing?"

How can you tell if a Brummy's been drinking?
He's got yellow pumps and a rusty zip.

The Warwickshire businessman had come to the National Exhibition Centre for a show, and was staying in a nearby hotel. Being away from home for the first time in ages, he decided to book a call-girl for the night.

A few minutes later, she arrived.

"How much is it going to be?" asked the businessman.

"How much have you got?" replied the prostitute.

Being rather cautious, the businessman hid his wallet

from her and looked inside.

"Only a fiver, I'm afraid," he said.

"Is that all?" replied the call-girl irritably. "Oh well, I'm here now. Let's get on with it."

After the action had taken place, the businessman was very well pleased, and decided to reward the girl rather more handsomely.

"That was great. Here's £10," he said handing her the money.

"But I thought you said you only had a fiver," she said crossly.

"That was before I knew you were a virgin," smiled the businessman smugly.

"You must be joking!" replied the prostitute. "If I'd known you had ten quid, I'd have taken my tights off."

There was a young lady from Leek
Whose sexual responses were weak.
At the point of orgasm,
She just gave a spasm,
Then a barely perceptible squeak.

A young wife from Bromsgrove was sick and tired of waiting for her husband to come back from the pub, and so decided that, in future, she would have a night out with the girls once a week. Her husband hated the idea and he was even more perturbed when she returned from her first hen night with a new mink coat.

"Where did that come from?" he demanded.

"Oh, I won it in a raffle," she replied casually.

The following week she went out again, this time returning with a diamond necklace.

"And where did that come from?" he asked her.

"Oh, I won it in a raffle," she said equally calmly.

The third week she was getting ready to go out when she shouted to her husband to prepare a bath for her.

"Okay, dearest," he replied sweetly.

A few minutes later he shouted up to her that it was ready. However, when she came down, although her perfume and talc had been laid out, she saw that the bath was empty save for half an inch of water.

"Why haven't you filled the bath properly?" she asked irritably.

"Well, I thought there might be another of those raffles tonight," her husband replied. "And you've been doing so well, I didn't want you to get your ticket wet."

Have you heard that Moseley is going to be the venue for the first Gay Male Church? But don't worry, it will be easy to spot if you've gone in there accidentally. Only half the congregation will be kneeling.

Overheard in a pub near the Bull Ring.
Girl: Oy what is it that makes me more attractive than other girls, Darren?
Man: Guess!
Girl: I give in.
Man: Got it in one.

Barbecues in the suburb of Greet
Are not for the shy or effete.
The girls serve the food,
Then strip to the nude,
Whilst the chefs stand beating their meat.

Brenda and Graham from Edgbaston had been married for
some months, but still Graham was far from being an
experienced lover. In fact, his impetuousness and speed
was beginning to get Brenda down, so she decided to give
him a few lessons in the art of love-making.

"You should move more gently, Graham," she
suggested as they lay in bed one night. "Your trouble is
that you go at it like a bull at a gate. Here! I've got an idea."

With that, she took out her purse and produced four
coins. Carefully she balanced a penny on both of his
shoulders, a tenpenny piece on the small of his back, and a
pound coin between his buttocks.

"Now what I want you to do, Graham, is move each of
the parts with a coin on in turn," Brenda suggested, "and
as you do so, say, 'Penny, penny, ten pence, pound.' You
got that?"

"Okay, bab," said Graham. "I'll give it a try like."

Then he started to make love, moving more slowly this
time.

"Penny, penny, ten pence, pound," he whispered as he
moved. "Penny, penny, ten pence, pound."

"Good, that's good," said Brenda, getting worked up
for the first time in their marriage.

"Penny, penny, ten pence, pound," he continued
breathlessly.

"Oh yes, yes," panted Brenda.

"Penny, penny, ten pence, pound," he cried, his voice growing louder with the excitement.

"Go on, go on," screamed Brenda.

"Penny, penny, ten pence, pound. Penny, penny, ten pence, pound. Penny, penny – oh sod it! £1.12, £1.12, £1.12."

Overheard in a back street in Sandwell.

"Daddy, what are those two dogs doing?"

"Well, son, one's broken down, so his friend is pushing him to a garage."

The Post Office have announced that they are issuing special stamps to commemorate 200 years of prostitution in Balsall Heath. The commemorative stamps will be 18p each, but it will cost an extra 5p to lick them.

Two Birmingham city footballers were changing after a match when one noticed that their centre forward was wearing a rather unusual jockstrap.

"Hey, I've never seen one like that before," he remarked. "Where did you get it?"

"Oh it's a new one made by Austin Rover in Longbridge," the centre forward replied.

"Really? Is it any good?"

"No," said the player irritably. "It drives me nuts."

For ten years Jeff and Wally had supported the Villa, occupying the same place on the terraces. Then the team struck a bad patch. Home victories became further and further apart, and while Jeff carried on loyally waving his claret and blue scarf, Wally stayed at home.

One Saturday night after a miserable five-nil defeat at the hands of Everton, Jeff went into the pub near their homes in Perry Barr for a consolation drink. He'd just sat down in the corner when he noticed his old friend Wally leaning on the bar.

"Hi Wally, I don't see you at Villa Park much these days," said Jeff.

"No, the wife won't let me go."

"I know what you mean," said Jeff. "My missus used to be like that until I found the answer."

"What's that, Jeff?"

"I'd say, 'Excuse me, luv, do you mind if I go to see the Villa this afternoon?' and if she said she did, I'd pick her up, put her over my shoulder, take her upstairs, throw her on to the bed, pull her knickers down and give her a good spanking until she said I could go. You should try it, Wally."

"Okay, I will."

The next Saturday afternoon, Aston Villa lost three-nil to Manchester United. Standing waving in support was Jeff but not Wally. Again Jeff decided to drown his sorrows in a few pints of Ansells Mild in his local, and again he bumped into Wally.

"I thought you were coming to the match today?" Jeff said.

"I was but the wife wouldn't let me."

"But I thought you were going to do what I do."

"Oh I did," sighed Wally. "I said 'Do you mind if I go and watch the Villa this afternoon, dear?' and she said she did. So I picked her up, put her over my shoulder, took her upstairs, threw her on the bed and pulled her knickers down. Then I thought...bugger it, they haven't been playing very well recently, have they?"

A man in a bus queue in Stoke,
Unzipped his flies for a joke.
An old man gave a shout
And almost passed out,
Whilst a lady nearby had a stroke.

Two posh but bitchy ladies from Sutton Coldfield turned up at the funeral of a friend to shed mock tears. Much to their disgust, she had had no less than eight husbands and outlived them all, so died alone.

"Oh well, at least they will be together again in heaven," said one, wiping away non-existent tears with a lace hanky from Rackhams.

"Yes, that's right," replied the other with a theatrical sob. "But with which husband?"

"No, no, my dear," said the first. "I was referring to her legs."

What happens if you don't tip the dustman in Small Heath?
He stops delivering.

How can you tell when a Solihull girl has had an orgasm?
She drops her packet of crisps.

A Walsall man went to the doctor complaining that he
could no longer satisfy his wife when they made love.

"Don't worry," the doctor told him, "it happens to a lot
of men your age. I'll give you some tablets, but be careful
they're quite strong. Don't take more than two, will you?"

Come bedtime, the man got the jar of pills out and
started to take a couple. Then he thought for a moment.

"That doctor doesn't realise I haven't made love for six
months, I'd better take a couple more," he said to himself.

Then he thought again.

"And my wife is a hard woman to satisfy. I'd better take
a couple more to be on the safe side," he said as he
swallowed a further two.

"...And she likes it more than once," he added, and
wolfed down another four pills.

Climbing into bed he felt better than he ever had before.
He was 18 again and bursting with desire. Much to his
wife's surprise, he leapt on top of her and made love to her
passionately and highly satisfactorily. Then he did it again
– and again and again. By one in the morning she was
exhausted, and fell asleep happier than she could ever
recall. However, at three she woke up and found herself
alone.

"Bernard!" she shouted, but there was no reply.

So she put her dressing gown on and went downstairs.
Walking into the lounge, there was their dog lying on the
floor wagging its tail and panting happily, but no sign of
Bernard. She went into the kitchen. There was the cat

looking slightly ruffled but purring contentedly, but still no sign of Bernard. Then she spotted a light on in the garden shed. She put on some shoes and went outside. As she opened the shed door, she saw a most unusual sight. There was her husband with his tool in the vice about to attack it with an electric sander.

"Bernard!" she cried. "Whatever are you doing?"

Her husband swung around.

"Well," he said. "You've had enough and you're happy. The dog's had enough and he's happy. Even the cat's had enough and she's happy. I'm buggered if I'm gonna let our budgie down."

An East Midlands firm held their annual sales conference in the Hilton Hotel at Stratford. The mood was buoyant as sales had been up on the previous year, and long celebrations were held in the bar. One particularly cocky man had just been named salesman of the year, and was drinking champagne and boasting loudly. Then suddenly he was approached by a rather stern man.

"Excuse me but are you Joe Weston?" he asked.

"Sure am, squire," replied the salesman. "What can I do for you, me old mate?"

"Tell me, Mr Weston, were you in the Birmingham area last month?"

The salesman took out his filofax.

"A month ago, now let me see," he mumbled as he flicked through the pages. "Yes, as a matter of fact I was, exactly a month ago today."

"And did you, by any chance, stay at the Holiday Inn?" the man asked.

"Hang on a mo," said the salesman looking more closely

at the entry. "Yes, that's right. Two nights at the Holiday Inn."

"And," continued the man getting more irritable, "did you have room 1089?"

"Just a – yes, room 1089, that is correct. Look what is this, bloody Mastermind?"

The man ignored him.

"And in the next room was a Mrs Hoskins, right?"

Again he consulted his filofax.

"As a matter of fact, yes -"

"And you slept with her, didn't you?"

The salesman turned the page.

"Er yes. That's right, I did."

"Well, Mr Weston," said the man angrily. "I am Mr Hoskins and let me tell you I don't like it."

Calmly the young man flipped to the back of his filofax, leafed through the pages and ran his finger down a list.

"Now let me see, Mrs Hoskins, Holiday Inn Birmingham, room 1089...no, neither did I."

An impoverished but good-looking Aston University student had been invited to a fancy dress party but it being the end of term had very little to spend on a costume. However, he went to the hirers to see what he could find.

"How much have you got exactly?" asked the lady assistant.

The student went through his pockets and eventually found a pound coin.

"Only a pound eh?" said the assistant. "Well, I can do you a fig leaf for 75p, and you could go as Adam. You certainly have the physique for it."

"Okay," he replied.

"What size are you – small, medium or large?"

"I don't know."

"Well, try the medium and see how you go," suggested the assistant.

The student went into the changing room and returned sporting a fig leaf evidently too small to hide his ample appendage.

"Oh, I see we need a large, sir," said the assistant, much impressed.

Again the student disappeared and returned with the bigger fig leaf in place, but it was still inadequate.

"Ooooh sir! It's still not quite big enough, is it?" grinned the girl. "And that's the largest we do, I'm afraid."

"Oh dear," said the student miserably.

"Hang on, I've got an idea."

With that the assistant disappeared into the store-room and returned carrying a white cardboard box with the word 'super' written on it.

"I've got just the thing for a man of your build," she told him. "Put this on your head and go as a petrol pump."

After years of being unemployed, Eddie got a job at a sleazy Midlands night club as a bouncer.

"Congratulations, Mr Harris," said the manager. "Now about pay. I can only offer you £90 a week here but you do get some excellent perks."

"Really?" replied Eddie. "Like what?"

The manager lent over and whispered in his ear.

"Well, between you and me," he said, "we rent the top rooms of the club to the local ladies of the night. In return, they give each of our staff a free bonk per evening."

"That's terrific," said Eddie.

"My advice is try a new one every night for the first week and then stick with the girl who pleases you most. That way we can arrange a satisfactory timetable."

"Okay, I will."

Eddie started work the following evening and as he stood at the door he couldn't help thinking about the delights that were to come. As soon as the club closed he went upstairs to the first room.

"Who is it?" came the reply as he knocked on the door.

"I'm Eddie the new doorman," he said.

"Okay, come in."

As he sat on the bed, the girl, dressed in a baby doll nightie, consulted a list, found his name and ticked it. Then she started unzipping his flies. Eddie could barely contain himself. However, when she just played with him until he'd come, he was a little disappointed. Nevertheless, he thought, there's another girl tomorrow, I'll try her.

The next day after work he went to the second room, knocked and went in. This time a blonde in a PVC basque and shiny black gloves consulted the list and ticked him off. Again he sat on the bed, and again he was disappointed when instead of having sex, she merely brought him off in her hand.

By the end of the week, he had tried five doors and five different girls but none had offered him more than a quick rub. As his new boss handed him his £90, he asked how he was getting on.

"Well, now you mention it," he said miserably, "you said I could have sex with any of the girls upstairs after work as a perk, but every time I go up there all I get is tossed off. It's a bit of a disappointment."

"I'm sorry, I should have told you," replied the manager. "We work a week in hand here."

Did you hear about the West Bromwich girl who bought matching luggage for her honeymoon? All her carrier bags came from the same supermarket.

A retired factory owner and his wife lived on a large estate near Henley-in-Arden looked after by several servants. However, when the stock market slumped, the old man realised that he would have to draw his horns in a bit.

"Now we need to get rid of some of the staff I'm afraid, dear," he said to his wife. "Now I can't lose my butler, my valet and my chauffeur, but if you could take up cooking again we could get rid of your kitchen maid."

"Oh yes, dear," she replied, a little irked by his selfishness, "and if you were to take up bonking again, we could get rid of the gardener."

It was three in the morning and everyone on the Coventry estate was asleep – except Paul.

"Hey, Judy, wake up, wake up," he said urgently to his wife. "Our house is haunted."

"Don't be ridiculous, Paul," said his wife sleepily. "It was only built by Barratts in 1984. It can't possibly be haunted. I told you not to have that last pint of Brew X1..."

"No, love, I'm serious," he replied breathlessly. "I've just had an experience that can only be explained by something from the other side."

"Okay, what happened?" asked his wife wearily.

"I went to the bathroom and as I walked in, the light came on without my touching the switch. Then, as I went out again, it went off without my touching it. It must be ghosts or poltergeists..."

"Oh God, Paul," said Judy with a sigh. "You haven't pissed in the refrigerator again, have you?"

THE NORTH EAST

Haway, the lads, it's the land of the Jolly Green Giro.
When it comes to unemployment, the North East has
bigger statistics than Sam Fox – only unlike Sam, theirs
aren't dropping. But Mrs Thatcher says that the Japanese
will save them, and already there's a Nip in the air. Nissan
have moved in so successfully in Sunderland, it's raining
Datsun cogs. But other areas aren't so lucky. In Stockton,
even the TSB likes to say 'No', and the Cashpoint machine
only gives out threats.

In Yorkshire, on the other hand, there are wealthy
farmers and even wealthier vets. People make a fortune
from relating how poor they were. I can't help wondering
why if Michael Parkinson likes Barnsley so much, he lives
in a big house on the Thames.

The humour, like the people, is blunt. Here it's
considered a virtue. Anywhere else, it's just bloody rude.

How can you tell a real Yorkshireman?
He jogs home from his vasectomy.

Little Annie was staying with her uncle and aunt in
Scarborough for the summer holidays. Bored one night,
she crept into their bedroom and for the first time in her
five-year long life caught a glimpse of her uncle's plonker.

"What's that?" she asked innocently.

"Ur it's an aerial," said Uncle rather feebly. "The aerial
to my new radio."

"It can't be that new," scoffed the little girl. "I heard
you say it was Ferranti."

Three elderly Yorkshiremen sat on a dry stone wall watching the local carnival procession go past. The brass band played, pretty girls from the villages on the moors danced and a good time was being had by all, except them.

"You know, age is a terrible thing," said Arkwright. "My hearing's so bad now, I can hardly hear t' band."

"Aye," agreed Allsop, "and my eyes are now so bad, I can hardly see those pretty little girls dancing."

Ernshaw, the third old man, sat silently. Then Arkwright turned to him.

"Eh up, Ernshaw, you're the oldest of t'three of us," he said. "You must be losing your faculties and all?"

"Happen you're right," he said, puffing on his pipe. "And I'm far worse off than you two."

"How do you mean?" asked Allsop.

"Only last night I was in bed with Noreen, the young barmaid from the Fox and Whippet, and I said, 'Ey, lass, how do you fancy making love?' and she said, 'You silly bugger, Ernshaw, we only made love ten minutes ago.' These days my memory's bloody awful..."

The wife of a mad-keen Yorkshire cricket fan was in the maternity hospital. Her husband, anxious not to miss a moment of the Roses match, was at home watching the television. His only contact with his wife was by phone. When bad light stopped play for a few minutes, he rang the hospital to find out how she was getting on.

"Has she had the baby yet?" he asked the sister of the maternity ward.

"Yes, Mr Boycott, she has, but there might be another on the way. Can you ring back in half an hour?"

Edward Boycott went back to the television. Half an hour or so later came the tea interval, so he rang again.

"Sorry, Mr Boycott, but there's another on the way," said the sister. "Can you ring back in another half an hour?"

He went back to the match. Half an hour later, just as the players were coming out on to the pitch, he rushed to the phone to ring the hospital again. Unfortunately, in his haste, he inadvertently rang the Test Score phone line instead.

"Can you tell me how my wife's doing?" he said to the recorded message.

"It's 125 all out," came the reply, "and the last one was a duck."

One for the ladies:
What do you call three Middlesbrough men doing the washing up?
A start.

Two Geordies were walking around Newcastle looking for ladies of the night. Neither being in work, they were searching for bargains, and were told of an American girl new to the area who was doing it for just five pounds. It wasn't long before the lads found her.

"So, how much is it, like?"

"Five pounds to you, darling."

The two Geordies hadn't heard an accent like it. She was obviously from a well-to-do family in California, and very naive. So they decided to try their luck.

"Five poond! Tha's a bit steep for roond here, lass. I wanna see wha am gettin' for me money first, pet."

"Why surely, sir," replied the innocent American politely.

With that she lifted her mini-skirt to reveal a neat little pussy, her pubic hair trimmed and laced with the beautiful fragrance of expensive perfume.

"Haway, that's a canny 'un," said the Geordie appreciatively.

Then to his great surprise the prostitute slapped him hard across the face.

"How dare you!" she cried.

"Whatever's the matter, pet?"

"Look, I may be new over here," she replied angrily, "but where I come from, a canyon is something big enough for cowboys to ride their horses through."

What do you call a Teessider in a suit?
The accused.

A young girl was hitchhiking on the A1 going north and prepared to do anything to get a lift, so when a large truck from Scunthorpe stopped and a handsome trucker beckoned her in, she was more than grateful.

"I've always wanted to get a lift from a driver as good-looking as you," she whispered, carefully crossing her stockinged legs to reveal lots of thigh. The driver just stared at the road and tapped the wheel in time to the country and western music on the radio.

"I'm more than willing to reward you for your help..." she continued, pulling her teeshirt taut over her breasts so he could see her pert nipples – which he chose to ignore.

"Muscular men like you always turn me on..." she said, running her hands over his shoulders and kissing and biting his ears and neck, then taking his hand and placing it carefully on her thigh. The driver just grunted.

"Why feel me," she went on. "I'm all hot and sticky between my legs."

Suddenly, the driver swerved on to the hard shoulder, slammed on the brakes, and swung around to face her.

"That does it, love," he shouted angrily. "If you've sat on my Yorkie bar, I'll kill you!"

It was a stormy winter's night on the Yorkshire moors, and inside the tiny stone cottage on the windswept escarpment, an elderly couple and their 19-year-old daughter sat huddled around a roaring fire. Then suddenly there was a knock on the door. The old man went to answer it, and found on the doorstep a very bedraggled young man.

"Thank God you're in," said the stranger. "I've been walking for hours and I'm lost. Can I rest here until the storm subsides?"

"Course you can, lad," said the old man. "Come in and warm yourself by the fire."

The young man gratefully accepted the invitation, and joined the old lady and the attractive blonde girl by the fire.

"Eee where are my manners?" said the old man. "Let me introduce t'family. This is my wife, Ethel, and our Ida.

She's a student in Sheffield and come down for t'weekend. Look, why don't you have a glass of scotch with us?"

Again the young man gratefully accepted, and they sat together and talked for some time. Then the old man yawned and looked through the curtains.

"T'storm's still bad, son. I suggest you stay here the night. You can easily sleep on t'sofa. We don't mind. But if you'll excuse me, I'll be getting to bed."

Shortly after, his wife and their daughter went to bed too, leaving the young man alone on the sofa.

A couple of hours passed and the wind blew so hard it woke the old couple up.

"Eee that young man must be freezing," said the old man. "I'll go and see if he needs a blanket."

So he went downstairs to the lounge.

"Excuse me," he said to the young man asleep on the sofa. "I just wondered if you needed a blanket?"

"No, thanks," came the sleepy reply.

"What about a hot water bottle?"

"No, it's okay."

"In that case, how about having our eiderdown?'

"My God," said the young man, "I've heard of Yorkshire hospitality but this is ridiculous. She's been down twice already."

"You think more about food than you do about sex," nagged the wife of the Bradford businessman as he munched his way through a second helping of Yorkshire pudding.

"Whatever do you mean, love?"

"We must be the only people in the country with mirrors on the ceiling of the dining room."

Piece of graffiti spotted in the toilets of one of the new Japanese-run factories in Sunderland.

"Japanese bosses are like blisters. They're small, yellow and only show up after the work's been done."

The owner of a small tailor's shop in Goole was woken at 3 am by the phone ringing.

"Hello?"

"Mr Johnson?"

"That's right."

"Hello, it's Jack Baker from next door."

"What do you want at this time of night?"

"I'd like you to know. I've just taken your daughter to bed and bonked her for three hours solid. She's terrific."

"So what's that to do with me? She's 28 now. She can look after herself."

"I just wanted to congratulate you. I've been getting things from your shop for 25 years, and this is the first thing you've made me that fits."

A butcher from York went to see his GP about a rather unfortunate sexual tendency.

"Er, excuse me, doc," he said, "but I don't exactly know how to tell you this."

"Don't worry, you can be frank with me," replied the medico.

"But you see, I keep getting this terrible temptation to put my sausage in the bacon slicer."

"My God! You mustn't do that," exclaimed the doctor. "You could do yourself serious damage."

"I can't help it. I just know one day I'll give in and do it."

"Obviously you're suffering from stress of some sort," suggested the GP. "Take these tablets four times a day, and come back and see me in a month."

"Aye, okay," said the butcher.

A fortnight later, the butcher was back in the doctor's surgery again.

"I said a month," the doctor complained. "The pills won't have had a chance to work yet."

The butcher was almost in tears.

"It's too late, I've done it!" he sobbed.

"You've put your thing in the bacon slicer?"

The butcher nodded.

"Good God! Are you all right?"

The butcher nodded again.

"I'm fine, doc," he said with tears in his eyes. "But now the bacon slicer's handed in his notice..."

After a few pints, the Grimsby trawlerman decided to have a tattoo done, so he went to a tiny parlour on the coast.

"And what exactly does sir want?" asked the lady tattooist.

Seeing the big blonde, the trawlerman was eager to impress her with his bravery.

"I'd like a giant eagle tattooed on me balls," he slurred.

The blonde, being well used to shows of drunken courage, smiled sweetly.

"Certainly, sir," she replied. "I'll get my ball point pen."

Leeds' drum majorettes are the best.
They march whilst getting undressed.
And what do they play
As they're stripping away.
Air on a G-String? You guessed!

The vicar of the small parish of Draughtdale was cycling
along when he saw a pretty little girl with a huge black cat.

"Ah hello, my dear, what a lovely cat!" he said. "What
do you call him?"

"Cooking fat," she replied innocently.

"Cooking fat, that's an odd name. How did he come by
that?"

"Me Dad gave it him when he tripped him over this
morning."

How can you spot a level-headed Yorkshireman?
His pint dribbles out of both sides of his mouth.

Young Sidney was out with his girlfriend in Newcastle and
after a few pints of 'Broon' began feeling a bit porky. So he
started sliding his hand up her skirt and into her knickers
in full view of the rest of the bus passengers.

"Away, Sidney, have yer nea manners?" she protested.
"I've told yer before, like. It's tits forst, man."

Leeds businessman Arnold Fairbrother came out of the executive toilet and smiled confidently at his secretary. What he didn't realise was that he had neglected to do up his flies – though the pretty blonde behind the typewriter spotted it immediately.

"Er excuse me, sir," she said as discreetly as possible. "I think you've left the garage doors open."

"Impossible," he replied. "I came to work by train this morning. I can't have done. Besides, how would you know? Sharon, just get on with that letter to Blagwells Bolts of Bradford, eh?"

"Yes, sir," said the sweet little girl.

At lunchtime, Fairbrother met his colleagues in the pub for a lager and sandwich as usual.

"You've got a wonderful secretary there, you know, Fairbrother," said one suddenly. "I wish I had her."

Arnold smiled.

"Yes, I agree. Mind you I think the strain's beginning to tell. She said something most peculiar about my garage doors being open this morning. God knows what she meant."

The colleague laughed.

"She meant your flies are undone, Fairbrother – and they still are, you silly bugger!"

Arnold blushed deep red, then hastily adjusted the neglected area. To hide his embarrassment, he drank rather more than usual, and was quite pissed by the time he got to the office. As he walked in, he remembered the incident in the morning, and decided in his drunken haze to try and make the best of it.

"Ah Sharon," he said, full of bottled courage. "You know when you said I'd left the garage doors open this morning. I knew what you meant really. It was my little joke. In fact I did it deliberately to show you the sleek red

L.B.T.O.B. – 5

Jaguar hard-top that's lurking inside just waiting to take you for a ride."

Sharon looked surprised.

"Oh really?" she said.

"That's right, Sharon. Did you see it there ready to roar

"No, I can't say I did," replied Sharon matter of factly. "It must have been hidden by the small Volkswagen with two flat tyres."

Meanwhile back in Leeds, a brash middle-aged businessman had finished 'working late' with his beautiful blonde secretary. He was just pulling up his trousers when the secretary looked down at him.

"Excuse me, sir," she said. "Do you mind if I ask a personal question?"

"Fire away, lass," said the cocky MD.

"How come you're grey and balding up top, but downstairs you're still fair?"

"There nowt remarkable about that," said the self-confident businessman. "That part of me's never had a worry in its life."

In the gardens of a row of back-to-back terraces, the washing lines were strung out like dismal bunting. On one line, the middle-aged mother's giant bloomers hung next to her daughter's tiny satin panties. A conversation started.

"Oooh, I saw a lovely film last night," said the

enormous wool bloomers. "It was called *An Officer and a Gentleman*. It was so romantic."

"How did you manage to see that?" asked the satin panties.

"Well, when Mrs Hardcastle is full of popcorn and chocolates she slumps in the seat, and sometimes her legs come apart and I get to peep out and see the movie."

"You're lucky," moaned the panties. "My owner goes to the cinema three times a week with her boyfriend. But she never thinks of taking me."

A piece of graffiti found in a tiny pub on the moors.
"What's the difference between a pig and a fox?
About six pints."

Did you hear about the Yorkshire farmer who was so big that when he died, they couldn't find a coffin large enough to bury him? In the end, they gave him an enema and put him in a shoe box.

Two old Yorkshiremen were walking through the park on a hot summer's day when they saw a girl sunbathing nude. The only thing hiding her modesty was a roofing tile from a local building site, placed strategically between her legs.

"Bloody 'ell, Alf," said one. "Times really have changed. I remember when they used to be thatched."

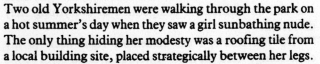

A hooker from Hull city centre
Refused to let pimps represent her.
She managed instead
With a sign by her bed
Saying, 'Darling, please pay as you enter.'

On a ferry out in the North Sea,
Jane confessed that it hurt her to pee.
"Oh God!" cried First Mate,
"That accounts for the state
Of the Captain, four stewards and me!"

What do you call three Whitby landladies up to their necks
in cement?
Not quite enough cement.

Another three elderly men (there are a lot of them about)
were walking across the dales chatting idly about anything
that came to mind. Rivals from schooldays, though, there
was still an element of competition in everything they
discussed.

"Do you know, I can remember right back to my
christening," said the first. "I were all dressed up in t'robe
and taken to this church where t'Vicar splashed water on
me."

"Aye, so can I," responded the second. "But that's nowt. I remember being in t'womb. It were lovely and warm, then I were squeezed through this right tiny hole into bright daylight."

"And so can I!" replied the third. "But that's nowt either. I remember going on a picnic on t'Dales with me Dad – and coming back with me Mam."

On the Tyneside council estate, few had jobs and money was scarce, so when the rentman came calling most pretended to be out. Nonetheless, he carried on, and knocked at Mrs Bramwell's door. There was no reply. However, when he put his ear to the door he could hear heavy breathing from the other side.

"Okay, Mrs Bramwell, I know you're there, open the door," he said.

"Who is it?" replied Mrs Bramwell panting hard.

"The rent man."

"Oh. Look, can you call back in half an hour? You've caught me in the middle of paying me grocery bill."

Three sisters from Middlesbrough, Jill, Marie and Fanny, were always on the look-out for new boyfriends. They hung around all the local discos. However, their dancing skills were hampered by having enormous feet. Jill's were size eight, Marie's size ten, and Fanny's a wopping size twelve.

One night Marie and Jill decided to leave Fanny behind, and go to the disco on their own, hoping they might be more successful. Sure enough, within minutes they were dancing with two eligible Stockton lads. All was going well until they were walking home as a foursome.

"Hey up, I've just noticed something," said one of the Stockton lads. "Haven't you two got big feet?"

Marie responded immediately.

"Huh! If you think they're big, you should see our Fanny's."

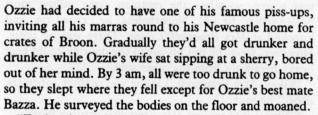

Ozzie had decided to have one of his famous piss-ups, inviting all his marras round to his Newcastle home for crates of Broon. Gradually they'd all got drunker and drunker while Ozzie's wife sat sipping at a sherry, bored out of her mind. By 3 am, all were too drunk to go home, so they slept where they fell except for Ozzie's best mate Bazza. He surveyed the bodies on the floor and moaned.

"Ee there's nowhere left to sleep, like. Where do I go?"

"That's okay, marra," replied Ozzie, "you can sleep with us. There's plenty of room for three in our bed."

"If you're sure, like..."

"Aye, Mary won't mind."

So they all fell into the double bed, Mary crushed between the beer-filled friends. At five in the morning, Mary woke up and decided to make the most of the opportunity. She nudged her husband's mate.

"Eh Bazza?" she said. "How do you fancy a bit while Ozzie's asleep? You know I've always fancied you as much as him. And he won't wake up for hours yet."

Bazza woke up hardly believing his ears.

"Well, alreet, if you're sure he's asleep."

"I'll prove it to you," she said. "Look."

And with that she lowered the bedclothes to reveal his

bare bum. Carefully she took a hair on his left buttock between her fingers and pulled it sharply. Ozzie grunted but didn't wake.

"There, does that prove it?"

"Okay then," said Bazza, and very gently started to make love. It was quiet but quick and only a couple of minutes later, both were enjoying a long climax.

"Eeee, that were just how I imagined it," said Mary. "Let's do it again."

"But what if he wakes up..." said Bazza, still concerned.

"He's just as fast asleep as he was," insisted Mary. "Look." And with that she plucked another hair from his bottom without him even flinching.

"Right, off we go then," said Baz, and this time a little more recklessly they bonked for a good few minutes.

"Ooooh Bazza, Bazza, again, again," panted Mary.

"But Ozzie, he might -"

"Oh no he won't," she said and again pulled a hair from his bum. This time though there was a long grunt and a muffled sleepy voice.

"Bazza?" said Ozzie, still half asleep.

"Yes what is it, Oz?" said Bazza nervously.

"Look, pal," he mumbled. "I don't mind you banging me wife, but do you mind telling her not to use me arse as a scoreboard?"

A Yorkshire supporter called Rees
Watched the game with his girlfriend, Denise.
But the John Player League
Never held the intrigue
Of his bat and two balls at her crease.

At the office Christmas party, the staff of the Doncaster firm were celebrating the forthcoming holiday with great verve and considerable alcohol. In a corner sat three of the top salesmen in cheap suits boasting about their sexual expertise.

"I always go for older women myself," said the first, a pimply 20-year-old. "More expertise in the sack. Only last week I had a fabulous time in a hotel with the receptionist who was pushing forty."

"That young eh?" said his colleague, much the same age. "A month ago in Bradford, I was up all night with a housewife who was 46, and brilliant at it. What about you, Bernie?"

"Oh, the best I've done was shag a 30-year-old," he replied.

The others scoffed.

"Bernie, you don't know what you're missing!"

"Oh yes I do," he said with a faraway look in his eye. "I was only 12 at the time."

The owner of a string of second-hand car showrooms in Teesside decided to go to a massage parlour that had been recommended to him for their 'special services'. After easing away his tensions with a standard massage, the girl asked if he would like a little 'extra' in the form of some hand relief.

"Aye, I would, lass," he replied. "But I'm not paying extra, mind, I've a business to support."

"I'm sorry, sir, the charge is £20," replied the masseuse, shocked by the meanness of the obviously well-off old man.

"In my trade, we believe in bargaining. Make it £10, and I'll throw in a free test drive of my car of the month."

Rather than lose the business, the girl was forced to agree. As she started, the car dealer smiled smugly.

"Ay, you know this isn't just any old pud your pulling, lass," he boasted. "This is the most powerful model in Teesside. When I let off, I don't just come – I explode – and you'd better stand back! But don't worry, I'll shout when it's gonna happen!"

The masseuse managed to keep a straight face, and carried on. Within a few seconds, he let out an enormous yell.

"Stand back!!"

The masseuse stayed where she was. Instead, she calmly put her finger over the top of his member.

"Okay, marra," she said tersely. "I've got a business to support and all. Make it the full £20, or I'll blow your balls to bits."

THE NORTH WEST

The North West is an area of contrasts. From Blackpool rock to Liverpool on the rocks, humour is never far away. Just look at the entertainers who've come out of the North West. Arthur Askey, Jimmy Tarbuck, Cilla Black – with acts like that around you need a sense of humour.

One thing is no laughing matter though – football. The North West play it better than anywhere else in the world. Man United may sound like a gay fantasy, but they're one of our greatest teams. It's a little known fact that I once had a trial with United – they took me to court for parking on the yellow lines outside the main entrance.

Enough of all this though, it's time we Preston...

Being a cosmopolitan town, Liverpool was picked for the first inter-denominational congress on the subject of family planning. Representatives of religions all over the world attended, but unfortunately, the Roman Catholic had to pull out at the last minute.

A Radio Merseyside reporter was sent to interview a good Catholic lady who had just had a baby, her fifteenth, all of them boys. He switched on his tape recorder and started work.

"Hello and welcome to Birkenhead where I have with me, Mrs Edith Blackwell and her 15 sons. Now tell me, Edith, what's this little chap's name?"

"William," she replied immediately.

"And what about this one?"

"William," came the reply.

The reporter was a little bemused but being professional he carried on.

"So what about this little mite, eh?"

"Oh, he's William," replied the mother casually.

"Surely they're not all called William?" joked the reporter.

"Yeah, actually, they are," said the proud mum.

"But how on earth do you distinguish between them, say, if you want to call one of them in from the garden?"

"Oh, that's easy," she replied. "They've all got different surnames."

John from Morecambe was already late for work when the phone rang. He picked it up.

"I'm sorry, I think you have the wrong number," he said. "The weather forecast is 9383."

"Who was it?" shouted his wife from the kitchen.

"Wrong number, darling," he replied. "It was some berk wanting to know if the coast was clear."

A randy young man slapped a girl's bottom as she was walking through Lime Street station. She turned round to him angrily.

"Hey, what did you do that for?"

The young man grinned.

"Oh I'm sorry, love, I thought you were me mother."

"Impossible," replied the girl immediately. "I'm married."

"Hey, teach, I wanna piss!" came the cry from the back of the class.

"No, Jimmy," said the lady teacher from the Blackburn comprehensive. "We don't ask like that. Really, the language in this school is appalling. In future, I'd like you to say, 'I wish to urinate, please.' Okay?"

The following day, Jimmy cried out again.

"Hey, teach, I wanna piss."

"No, Jimmy, remember what I told you. The word to use is urinate. Now, Jimmy, give me a sentence with the word urinate in,"

The boy thought long and hard.

"I've got one."

"Good. That's what I like to hear. We're on our way to stamping out the terrible language in this school. What's your sentence, Jimmy?"

"Urinate, miss, but if your tits were bigger you'd be a ten."

Last Christmas Eve, Martin was walking home from a party in Toxteth when he tripped on the kerb outside his house. Falling forward he collided with the gatepost, which hit him right in the soft centre between his legs. A searing pain shot through his body, and a passer-by, spotting a man rolling in obvious agony, called an ambulance.

He was still in pain when he arrived in casualty, where they gave him a local anaesthetic and some very bad news.

"I'm afraid you've broken it," said the doctor as three nurses scurried away trying not to giggle.

"But that's not possible..."

"Oh, yes it is," said the doctor, "especially in cold weather. But don't worry, I can help you."

So saying the medico constructed a splint around Martin's damaged dribbler consisting of four pieces of wood held together with sticking plaster. They supported it perfectly if not very comfortably. The spluttering nurses then helped Martin back into his trousers and sent him home.

On Christmas Day, Martin's girlfriend Mary was due to come round to exchange presents. Mary was a sweet girl but she had never let Martin do any more than fondle her wobbly bits. However, despite this, as a special treat for Christmas, Martin had bought her her favourite perfume and a gold bracelet. She loved them.

"Oh Martin, thank you so much," she said, kissing him hard. "Now, it's time for your present. Shut your eyes!"

Martin did as he was told.

"Now, open them!"

Again he did as requested and saw the best gift he could ever have imagined. Mary was lifting up her skirt and pulling down her panties to reveal...now I'm sure you know what she was revealing.

"Martin, it's all yours, and it's untouched by human hand!"

Martin responded at once, undoing his flies.

"How about this then? Mine's still in the bloody box!"

One Southport lady's frigidity,
Approached post mortal rigidity,
Till you gave her a drink,
Then she'd suddenly sink
Into a stunningly sexual liquidity.

A little boy was playing pirates in his Warrington street when the vicar approached. He smiled at the boy with his eye patch, pirate hat and cardboard cutlass.

"And what are you doing, my son?"

"Me and my crew are fighting against the evil Spaniards," he replied with a snarl.

The vicar looked around but could see nobody else.

"So where are your buccaneers?" he asked.

"Where do you think?" he replied. "Under me buck'n hat!"

At St Greavsie's Comprehensive in Toxteth, a teacher was trying to impress on her pupils the value of having a good breakfast.

"Without a good start in the morning, the brain cannot absorb information," she claimed. "Take Watkins for example…"

The teacher turned to look at the beaming smug face of the school swot.

"Watkins, what did you have for breakfast?" she enquired.

"Two boiled eggs, muesli and additive-free prunes," he replied brightly.

"Excellent. Now tell me, what is the capital of the USA?"

"Washington, DC, miss."

"Very good, Watkins. See what I mean? Now you, Lavinia Bach-Garden, what did you have for breakfast?"

"Cook prepared kedgeree and devilled kidneys, miss."

"Fine, and where is the River Amazon?"

"South America, miss."

"Now, what about you, Scuddy?"

The teacher stared straight at a snivelling little boy with a runny nose and less meat on him than a butcher's pencil.

"Tell me, what did you have for breakfast?"

"A stale crust, miss."

The class giggled.

"A stale crust. Now we'll see what I mean," said the teacher confidently. "So, Scuddy, tell me if you possibly can, where you'd find the Indian border?"

"That's easy, miss," replied the child. "He's in bed with Mum. That's why I could only find a stale crust this morning."

Graffiti spotted in a ladies public convenience in Blackburn.

"Lancashire men are like toilets. They're either engaged or filthy."

Two middle-aged ladies from Huyton met for tea after not seeing each other for several years.

"Oh, Daphne, wherever have you been? I haven't seen you for ages."

"I went on safari to Africa, Elizabeth dear, but I had a terrible time."

"Really?" replied Elizabeth, secretly rather pleased.

"Oh yes, we went out into the jungle one day to shoot lions and suddenly I was attacked by a gorilla. It was seven foot tall and grabbed me from behind, then it started to rip all my clothes off. My dress – you know that lovely white one I bought two years ago – was torn to shreds, then he climbed on top of me and started to yank down my...well, you know."

"Oh how awful!"

"Yes, and then he – well, I won't say what, but it hasn't happened since Jeremy died. I was taken straight to hospital and kept there for six months."

"Were you hurt?"

"I should say so. In all that time he didn't write, he didn't phone..."

How do you bonk a fat Morecambe landlady?
Roll her in flour and aim for the damp patch.

A long-legged brunette in a minute mini skirt stood by the M6 trying to flag down trucks. Eventually one of them stopped.

"Can you give me a lift to Preston?" she asked with a seductive smile.

"Okay," said the trucker, "but it's a ride for a ride, love."

"That's all right," she said. "Just before the turning, we can get out and you can do what you like."

The girl was as good as her word and as the sign for Preston came into view, he stopped the truck and they both got out excitedly. Not being a particularly lavish vehicle, it wasn't equipped with beds, so they decided that the most comfortable and least public place for her to fulfil her end of the deal was underneath the lorry itself. So they climbed between the rear wheels, and the girl set to with a willingness even the truck driver found exciting. So much so that not only did they keep at it for some time, but it took a little while for the driver to notice the large pair of black shoes that were beside him, and the police officer they belonged to. Eventually he did and looked up.

"Hello, hello, hello," said the motorway patrolman. "Now what would you be doing?"

The trucker tried to think of a reasonable excuse.

"Er...I was just inspecting the clutch cables, officer. I think they are working loose."

"I see, sir," said the policeman. "In that case, I think you'd better take a look at the brakes while you're at it. Your lorry's 200 yards down the road."

Overheard on a doorstep in Kirby.

"Mummy, Mummy, it's the milkman! Have you got the money or shall I go out to play."

When his elderly and rather timid aunt died, Paul went to her home in Wilmslow but was astonished to discover the cause of death. She had suffered a heart attack while making love with two six-foot men whom she paid to come and 'service her' once a month.

"How can I tell all the relatives?" he asked the policeman called in to look into the suspicious death. "She was such a quiet, respectable woman. How can I say she died being shagged by two men simultaneously? They'd be mortified. And then there'll be the police reports in all the papers. Oh the scandal!"

"Don't worry about it, sir. I'm sure we can handle it," said the policeman. "It's not the first time. In fact we get lots of celebrities, MPs, judges and so-on dying in awkward circumstances. I'll use the standard phrase for a death of this sort."

"Oh, what's that?"

"Mrs Williams died contentedly at the stroke of two..."

Having always wanted to take an oriental girl to bed, Barry successfully got off with the daughter of the owner of his local Chinese take-away in Salford. He took her out for a drink and as she sat there in a tight dragon-patterned silk kimono he couldn't resist running his hand up her smooth thigh. Then as they got a taxi back to his house for coffee, he noticed the sheen of the material on her pert breasts and couldn't stop himself fondling them in the dark confines of the back seat. Even as she left the cab, he succumbed to the urge to grab her sweet little bottom and give it a playful pat.

Inside he made coffee, but it wasn't long before he had coaxed her into bed with him. Everything he ever fantasised about Eastern girls proved to be true. Her movements were beautifully fluid, she touched him as if he was delicate china, and their kisses were as sweet as the desserts she normally sold in her restaurant. In fact, Barry was having such a good time, by 3 am he had made love to her no fewer than five times, and was now lying back smoking a cigarette.

After a few puffs, he felt himself on the rise again.

"Do you know what I could do with now?" he said.

"No, what?" came the musical oriental voice.

"A quick 69 before we go to sleep."

To his amazement the girl sat up in bed angrily.

"Look," she said, her eyes flashing with irritation. "I don't mind we go for a drink and you grope my thigh in the pub. I don't mind we go home in a taxi and you fondle my breast. I don't mind you grab my bum as we get out. I don't even mind you make love to me five times in a row. But I'm not getting up and cooking at three in the morning!"

Another one for the ladies:

Graffiti reported from the ladies loo of a pub in Bolton.

"Why did God create Lancashire men?

Cos science hasn't come up with a vibrator that can cut grass."

The foreman of a small firm near Bolton was called in to see the management.

"I'm sorry to have to tell you this, but as you know times are hard here in the North West, and I'm afraid it's necessary to make two workers redundant. I thought you were probably the best person to decide exactly who leaves us."

The foreman racked his brain over the unenviable task. Who would suffer least from redundancy? Eventually he came to the conclusion that it would have to be Maureen Batley because her husband was working elsewhere and old Jack Hodge because he was due for retirement soon anyway. Decision made, all he had to do was tell them.

After spending the morning at work pacing nervously, he decided that the tea break would be the best time to break the bad news. Jack and Maureen always used the same tea machine, and he would be able to tell them together. Sure enough, at 11 o'clock, Maureen and the old man came over for their cups of tea.

"Hey, George, you look right miserable, wherever's the matter, kid?" asked Maureen, a bottle blonde with big boobs.

"I'm afraid I'm going to have to lay you and Jack off," replied the foreman.

"Sorry, love," replied Maureen. "I've got an 'eadache. But you're welcome to jack off behind one of the machines."

Have you seen Morecambe's illuminations this year? Red, amber, green. Red, amber, green...

An over-keen DHSS official was snooping on an unmarried couple he was convinced were members of the Black Economy, ie, working while claiming social security. Try as he might, he couldn't find anything to convict them on until, watching through their bedroom window with his binoculars, he spotted the claimant using a condom with a two-inch extension. Exhilarated, he knocked on their door.

"Yeah what is it?" demanded the young man angrily.

"I'm from the Department of Health and Social Security. I've been watching you in the bedroom. I saw what you're using and I'm having you charged with offences against the state."

"Whatever for?"

"In your case, Mr Watkins, for not getting planning permission to extend your property, and your girlfriend for failure to report a supplementary benefit."

Whenever he has clients to see
Manchester manager, Jim Lee,
Always travels by plane,
And if asked to explain.
Says, 'I just love TWA tea!'

It's a little known fact that Oldham was going to be the site of Britain's first all-Lesbian nightclub. Unfortunately, though, they couldn't get a licker licence.

Brian was staying in a guest house in Blackpool for his holidays but, in order to return with a tan to impress his friends, he was spending the afternoons on a sun bed. To give the impression he'd been at one of the naughtier resorts, he decided to slip his trunks off for an all-over tan. Unfortunately he succeeded in burning his member rather badly. When he told the owner of the solarium, he said the best thing to do was bathe it in milk, so the instant he got back to the guest house, he went into the kitchen.

There was no sign of the landlady, so he poured a large glass of milk and dipped his poor sore part in it. At that moment, the long-time widowed landlady walked in.

"Oh!" she said, somewhat startled. "I always wondered how men reloaded those things."

Spotted in a Merseyside cemetery, two graves next to one another. The first read,

"Here lies Mrs Ethel Brady cold as usual."

The next, obviously revenge by her friends on her husband's demise,

"And here lies Edward Brady – stiff at last."

A boring old man from the Wirral
Gave up any hope of being virile.
So he chopped of his nadgers,
Gave his dick to the badgers,
Then donated his nuts to a squirrel.

Overheard on a bus in Stockport.

"My Bert tried to put the magic back into our love life last night."

"Really?"

"Yeah, but his wand wasn't up to it."

An ex-Liverpool docker walked into his local Jobcentre.

"Er excuse me, pal, but do you have a job going?" he asked.

"Yes, sir," replied the assistant.

"You ought to get some sennapods then."

Des the DJ really fancied himself as he played records in a seedy Manchester nightclub. Dressed in a silver shirt, lamé trousers and weighed down with medallions he chatted up the girls as the music played.

"Hi, babe," he leered at a bottle blonde chewing gum as she danced.

She looked up, clearly unimpressed.

"Do you like the threads?" he asked.

"Yeah, great," replied the girl with a thick Liverpool accent and a great deal of sarcasm. "Tell me, is that shirt real silk?"

"Yeah, kid, it sure is," lied Des.

"I thought so," said the girl, still chewing her gum. "It's still got a worm in it."

A new cocktail bar opened in Manchester famous for its range of drinks and mixers. Eager to show off, a young man from London walked in and strode to the bar.

"What have you got?"

"What would you like?"

He thought long and hard, determined to find something the barman wouldn't have.

"I know, I'll have a whisky and hot milk."

"Certainly, sir."

And with that the barman called over a beautiful blonde barmaid who undid the halter neck of her dress, took out her left boob and after putting a shot of scotch into his glass, squeezed her nipple until it streamed milk into the drink.

"I say, that's jolly impressive. If I'd known you Northern johnnies served whisky and hot milk like that, I'd have left London years ago."

The barmaid looked askance.

"And if I'd known you were from London, love," she said irritably, "I'd have shown you how I do whisky and water."

Graffiti spotted in a pub near Manchester University.

"Make as many cutting remarks as you like about vasectomies but it's made a *vas deferens* to my sex life."

Two young girls were on holiday in Spain, and walking along the beach. As one took her top off, her friend noticed a large letter W on her stomach.

"Hey how did you get that?"

"Oh I met this English boy from university at the disco last night. Then we came to the beach and made love. Trouble was his teeshirt was damp and the lettering got transferred."

"Really? Where was he from? Warwick?"

"No, Manchester."

A Scouser walked into one of the new smart cafés being built in the long-dead docks. He surveyed the menu disconsolately and then summoned the rather prim waitress.

"Eh, luvver, I'll have a cup of tea, and how much is a slice of the gattucks?"

The lady winced.

"It's pronounced 'gatto', sir, and it costs £2.50 a slice," she said snootily.

The Scouser looked at her angrily.

"Oh, bollo to that then, I'll just have the tea."

A young couple decided to spend their honeymoon in the Lake District. It was a lovely warm summer's day and so they decided to make love in a pine forest. Slowly the husband began to strip off his wife's dress, then her bra and panties, then they rolled around on the bed of pine needles. Suddenly, she cried out.

"Ouch!"

"What's the matter, love?"

The husband looked down and saw that a pine needle had embedded itself in a very tender part of the girl's anatomy. Unable to see what she was doing, she asked her husband to take it out.

"I'm sorry I can't do that," he replied earnestly.

"Why ever not?"

"This is Forestry Commission land," he replied. "Didn't you read the sign?"

"What sign?" asked his wife, a little annoyed.

"The one over there that says, 'Do not remove timber from any recreational areas'."

Willy from Wigan spotted the pencil-slim blonde at the party. She was tall, elegant, and sophisticatedly beautiful.

"Hey, I fancy that," he said to his mate, looking at her bottom clad in skin-tight satin. "I'm chatting her up."

"No, Willy, you don't chat up girls like that. You use witty repartee," advised his friend.

"Witty repartee, watch this," he replied confidently. He sidled up to her.

"Hey, love, I've got a great joke for you," he said loudly as he closed in. "This one's so funny, it'll make your tits fall off."

The girl turned round revealing a low cut front with barely a bump inside it.

"Oh I see," said Willy. "You've heard it."

Max was having a miserable time at a party. It was full of his relatives from down south who were shouting about how wealthy they were. Eventually one of them came up to him.

"Hello, Max, old thing. Are you enjoying yourself?" he brayed.

"Yes, actually, I am," he replied. "It's the only thing here I can enjoy."

Dave, normally a regular in his local, dropped in for a quick one after an absence of some weeks.

"A pint of Tetleys, please," he demanded.

"Bloody hell, where have you been?" asked the barman.

"I haven't seen you for ages."

"No, I've been away down south at a two-week conference on reincarnation at the Hilton Hotel."

"Really," said the barman. "I didn't know you believed in that. It must have set you back."

"Aye, it did," replied Dave. "£800 to be precise. But I thought, what the hell, you only live once."

The young lady executive was desperate to get to her appointment in Carlisle and was belting up the M6 in her Porsche. The police gave chase and eventually caught up with her. They made her pull over on to the hard shoulder, then the police driver who rather fancied himself as the Sweeney Two, sidled up to the car.

"Okay, darling, where's the fire?"

The executive was wealthy, beautiful and in a terrible hurry. She had no time to waste on morons like this. Slowly she wiped her hair from her eyes, hitched her skirt to her hips to reveal eye-popping legs and dark brown stocking tops, and pointed to a pair of taut panties.

"Why officer, I'm sitting on it. How long a hose did you bring?"

It was Grand National Day at Aintree, and Scudder, a dedicated practical joker, decided it was time to entertain the crowds in his own way. So disguising himself as a race official, he sneaked into the course announcer's office and handed him a note he had prepared.

"Read this out, it's urgent," he insisted.

Without thinking the announcer turned on his microphone.

"And here's the latest on the betting," he read. "Lady Cynthia's Fanny has been scratched."

What the announcer didn't know was that far from being the name of one of the horses running in the National, Lady Cynthia was the wife of one of the VIP guests that day. However, his ignorance was soon to end. As soon as his announcement echoed over the tannoy, her husband burst into the office.

"What's the meaning of this?" he demanded angrily. "Lady Cynthia's Fanny isn't the name of a horse. That's my wife! Now put out an apology or I'll sue you for every penny."

"Yes, certainly, of course, my Lord," stumbled the announcer. Hastily he switched on the microphone.

"My apologies, lords, ladies and gentlemen," he said nervously. "A correction to the previous announcement. Lady Cynthia's Fanny has not been scratched. In fact, it's never been entered..."

SCOTLAND

For years, when it came to comedy, the only good thing to come out of Scotland was the 9.15 to King's Cross. Then came Billy Connolly whose aggressive Glaswegian humour made people laugh at the bits of their bodies that they'd always worried about before. Now he lives in the South East, doesn't drink and espouses vegetarianism. Oh well!

By tradition the English have bullied the Scots. They steal their homes to turn into farms, shoot their wildlife for pleasure and only show their television programmes on one night of the year. Ah Hogmanay! Auld Lang Syne and even older Andy Stewart's knees. A time when every Scotsman likes to get his hands on a smooth, golden brown 18-year-old, and feel it warm his whole body as it goes down. Yes, malt whisky – a drink that puts hairs on your sporran. What did you think I meant?

Many a time I've ventured north of the border, and loved every minute. And don't believe all that stuff about them being mean – except one landlady I stayed with in Inverness. She had a coffee vending machine in the lounge – honestly!

An English Conservative candidate was campaigning in the heart of Glasgow and not doing particularly well. In an effort to show that he was a 'man of the people' he went to the local red light district, and talked to the prostitutes about their problems. After a long discussion with one lady, he smiled insincerely and put his arms around her.

"So, I can rely on your vote then?" he said.

"Och no," she replied. "I never vote for anyone."

The Tory candidate was shocked.

"You never vote!" he exclaimed. "Why, madam, you are throwing away your rights as a resident of a democratic country. Everyone should vote, it's their birthright."

The prostitute gave him a wry smile.

"Look, pal, I've never worried about who gets in and screws me before so why should I bother now?"

Two men were walking in the Highlands when suddenly one was taken short and had to go for a piss. He hid behind a crag, but as soon as he started, an adder leaped out and bit him in a highly embarrassing place.

"Och Murray, Murray, come quickly, I've been bitten by a snake."

Murray rushed towards him.

"It's okay. I passed a phone box a couple of miles back. I'll phone for a doctor."

So saying, he walked as fast as he could to the phone box and dialled 999.

"Doctor, my friend's been bitten by an adder, can you come quick?"

"Where are you?"

"Just south of Ben Nevis."

"Oh God! It'll take hours to get there," said the doctor. "It could be too late. You'll have to do something yourself, otherwise he'll die."

"What have I got to do?"

"It's simple. You bite the infected area and then very carefully suck the poison out. If you don't, I'm afraid he'll never make it until I arrive."

Murray walked back to his friend, thinking about what he had to do to save his life. When he got there, his friend was rolling in agony on the ground.

"Murray, thank God, did you get through to the doctor?"

"Aye, Murray, I did."

"And what did he say?"

"You're gonna die."

After being on an oil rig for weeks, Jim McTavish finally returned to his native Aberdeen on a Friday night. Desperate for a woman he went straight to the red light district and found himself a stunning redhead. He went straight to her room and started undressing. Then they both fell on the bed. Jim was just about to make love to her when he stopped dead.

"What's the matter?" asked the prostitute.

"I think you'd better go to the toilet."

"Whatever for?" she asked, "I've only just been."

"I dare say," said Jim. "But you won't get another chance till Tuesday."

Wee Hamish was mean from the day he was born, and never generous enough to take girls out, relied on Glasgow prostitutes to relieve his frustrations. After much haggling, he eventually found one prepared to make love to him for the £20 he had saved.

"Thank you, lassie, but you'll have to excuse me, I'm rather shy," Hamish told the girl. "Do you mind if we do it in complete darkness and silence?"

"You're the customer," the prostitute replied. "Whatever you prefer."

Four hours later she was bonking away for no less than the fifteenth time, and heading for the sixteenth. She had been amazed by his stamina but kept the vow of silence until now.

"Och come on, Hamish," she panted. "Enough is enough, you've more than had your £20 worth."

An unexpectedly deep voice responded.

"I'm not Hamish, I'm Jimmy," came the reply.

"So where's Hamish?" demanded the prostitute.

"Hamish? Hamish?" thought Jimmy for some time. "Och I know. He must be the man outside selling the £10 tickets."

How was copper wire discovered?
Two Scotsmen fighting over the same penny.

How was the Tamar valley formed?
The winning Scotsman dropping it down a rabbit hole.

An old Aberdonian of nearly 80 was sitting on the patio on a warm summer's day watching his wee grandson playing. He looked down to see that the boy was staring intently at something in the grass.

"What are you looking at, laddie?" he asked.

"A worm, Grandad," replied the little boy.

"Why? What's it up to?"

"Och, it's crawling down its hole."

The canny old Scotsman smiled.

"I'll tell you what, little' un. I bet you 50p you cannea pull that worm out of its hole before it disappears. Are you on?"

"Okay, Grandad.",

Immediately the little boy pounced on the worm and pulled its tail as hard as he could, then proudly held the creature aloft.

"Ah! You won fair and square," said the old man handing over the 50p, "but I bet you a pound you cannea get him back doon again."

The boy still triumphant from his success fell into the trap.

"You're on, Grandad," he replied.

The old man smiled as the boy tried unsuccessfully to prod the worm back into its hole. He chuckled to himself and shut his eyes, then drifted off to sleep. A little while later he was awoken by a tug at his trouser leg.

"Grandad! Grandad! I've done it!" came an excited voice.

The Scot opened his eyes and watched the little boy take the worm and slide it straight down the hole. He looked harder and saw that the creature was no longer soft and wriggly but as straight and firm as a pencil.

"My pound, please, Grandad," he said excitedly, having learned about the joy of money from his old grandfather.

"However did you do that, me lad?" asked the old man.

"It was simple. I sprayed it with hair lacquer and it went hard and slid in easily."

"Oh, I see," replied his grandfather thoughtfully. "Hang on there, I'll just nip indoors and get your pound."

The little boy waited expectantly but instead of only taking a couple of minutes, the old man didn't return for fully half an hour. When he did, the little boy rushed to greet him.

"Grandad, have you got my pound?"

The old man chuckled happily.

"Oh aye, I've got your pound, sonny," he said, "and your grandmother would like you to have another five from her."

Jamie took a young girl back to his flat after a night in the local pub, and began fondling her.

"Now you be careful, Jamie," she remonstrated. "I'm no a whore, do you ken?"

Jamie looked flabbergasted.

"Who said anything aboot paying?"

A recent poll by a Scottish brewery asked if men had to get up in the night and why. Of those who said they did, 3 per cent said that they had to get up to go to the toilet, 2 per cent said they had to get up to go for a drink of water, and 95 per cent said they had to get up to go home.

An Edinburgh businessman was travelling home on the Inter-City sleeper one night. Slowly he climbed into the top berth, but unfortunately, as he did, his toupee fell off, and slipped into the bed below. Unbeknown to him, the lower berth was occupied by a blonde from Kilmarnock who was sound asleep, as the businessman began groping around blindly trying to feel for his wig.

At last, he felt something furry beneath his fingers. As he tried to pick it up, he heard a low moan and a female voice. He was startled.

"Ooooh yes, go on, go on," she said breathlessly, deep in a beautiful sensuous dream.

The businessman continued trying to pick up what he believed to be his toupee, only succeeding in fingering it more and more.

"That's it," the girl moaned. "Go on, it's yours, it's yours."

The businessman withdrew his hand quickly.

"I'm sorry, madam, you're mistaken," he replied curtly. "I always part mine down the side."

On the day the divorce became final Mrs McBride sat recalling her life with her ex-husband. He had been a complete bastard who hit her when he came back from the pub, regularly stole her money and was frequently too drunk to make love. After a little while, she decided what she needed now was the love of a good man, and thought the best thing to do was to place an advertisement in the local paper. A week later, it appeared.

"Divorcee seeks new man," it read. "Mustn't be violent or steal, but must be a good lover. Apply in person: 23 Highland Avenue."

No sooner had the advertisement hit the news stands than Mrs McBride's doorbell rang. She opened it and to her surprise found a kilted gentleman in a wheelchair with his arms and legs encased in plaster.

"Hello, I'm Geordie MacPherson," he said. "I've come

about your ad in the paper."

"But your arms are in plaster," said Mrs McBride, unable to hide the shock in her voice.

"Correct! So I cannea possibly hit you."

"Well no, I suppose not," she replied. "But your legs are in plaster too."

"Indeed!" he said with a smile. "So I cannea run off with your money."

"Oh! I see, but I need a good lover. Can you manage?"

"Why certainly," replied Geordie confidently. "How do you think I rang the doorbell?"

Two babies from a small fishing village on Skye were in their prams parked by the harbour. In their own language they were discussing the problems of being very young.

"Och it's terrible," said the first. "All I ever get is milk from a bottle."

"You want to try breast feeding," said the second sarcastically. "That's even worse."

"But I was always told that milk from the breast tasted better."

"Not if you share it with a man who smokes St Bruno."

Orcadian Willy Le Dunn was making his first trip to London.

"Now make sure you look after yourself," said his doting mother. "We don't want you disappearing like your brother Neil. He went down there and hasn't written or phoned for over two years."

"Why don't you give me his address and I'll get him to drop you a line when I'm down there," suggested Willy.

"Okay," replied his mother, looking through her wee address book, "It's London WC2."

"Do nea worry, I'll find him," said Willy confidently.

Willy arrived at Euston the following evening, and decided the first thing he ought to do was search for his long-lost brother. London was bigger and busier than he had expected and he thought he was never going to find him until he saw a sign on the station saying WC.

"Greet," he thought. "I've found London WC. Neil must be in there somewhere."

So he went in. Public toilets being rare in the Orkneys, this was Willy's first time in one, so he didn't recognise exactly what it was. To him the numbered cubicles looked like little houses.

"Aha," he thought when he spotted the cubicle numbered two. "London WC2. This must be the place."

So he rapped sternly on the door. An aggressive voice replied.

"Yeah. What is it?"

"Excuse me," said Willy politely. "Are you Neil Le Dunn?"

"Yeah," came the response, "but there's no paper."

"Huh!" tutted Willy with contempt. "That's no excuse for not writing for two years."

The Campbells, the couple next door
Are over-sexed people, I'm sure.
From the feminine shrieks
And the way the bed creaks,
The Campbells are coming once more.

A young and attractive female spectator, watching the Braemar Highland Games, approached a huge kilted caber tosser, smiling in awe.

"Tell me something, is anything worn under that kilt?" she asked.

"Och no," replied the Scot. "Have nea fear, it's all in perfect working order."

A young Erdington couple were planning to marry but didn't know the facts of life, so they went along to their doctor for an explanation. He tried to put it simply but no matter what he said he was met with blank faces. Finally in desperation the doctor pulled the girl onto the floor, ripped off her clothes, and made love to her in front of her future husband's eyes.

"There!" said the doctor. "That's what you do! Now are there any questions?"

"Er yes, Doc," said the young man. "How often do I have to bring her in, like?"

When Turpin and his sidekick Swift Nick
Held up a coach north of Wick,
An old maid inside
Triumphantly cried
"At last! I've been stuck up by Dick!!"

A small Highland village was cut off for several weeks and supplies in the local shop were running low. By the end of the third week, the only meat Mrs Mack could sell was dog meat, and locals were forced to eat that. Then eventually supplies got through.

"Hello, Mrs Mack," said Mrs McMasters, the first customer of the morning. "I'll have two tins of dog food, please."

"Och, you do nea have to worry about that now," said the shopkeeper, "we've got some fresh meat in."

"I dare say, but my husband has got quite used to it now. In fact he rather likes it."

"Won't it make him ill?"

"Och no!"

"Well if you're sure," said Mrs Mack and gave her the two tins.

Mrs McMasters came in every day that week, and continued buying the dog food. It wasn't until Saturday that it was notably absent from her order.

"You're no having the dog food, then?" said Mrs Mack.

"No, Bill's in hospital," said Mrs McMasters sadly.

"I'm sorry to hear that," replied Mrs Mack. "But didn't I say that the dog food would make your husband ill?"

"Och, it wasn't the dog food that's put him in hospital, Mrs Mack," she replied. "He slipped a disc last night."

"Oh really, how did he do that?"

"Bending over, trying to lick his balls."

What's the most successful oral contraceptive in Aberdeen?
"No!"

At a Hogmanay party sweet Sue
Invited two men for a screw,
So that as midnight tolled,
Out went the old,
And instantly in came the new.

A gardener called Kenneth McLear
Likes plants more than women, we fear.
'He's hardy perennial,'
Say folks who know Kenny well,
'He only comes up once a year.'

In a Glasgow night club, a former pop star and the
one-time manager of Cowdenbeath sat drinking and
recalling the days when they were well known. Then
suddenly out of the blue a beautiful blonde walked up to
them, undid her blouse, took off her bra and wobbled her
enormous boobs at them.

"I know you two," she cried. "You had a hit in 1973 and
you're the man who helped Cowdenbeath to the third
round of the Scottish FA Cup. Can I have your
autographs?"

Flattered beyond belief, the two men got out their pens
and two pieces of paper.

"No!" she protested. "I want you to sign my boobs!"

It was a strange request but she sat down between them,
and the has-beens went to work. The pop star tried
desperately to sign her left breast but his pen skated along

the smooth white surface, and the result was a splodgey mess. The football manager on the right-hand side was having no trouble at all. He held her mammary firmly in his hand, and wrote his name large across the front, using the nipple to dot the I. The pop star was puzzled.

"Hey, how come when I write on her left boob, it all blots and runs, yet when you sign the other side, it comes out perfectly?" he asked.

The football supremo smiled.

"That's easy," he replied. "You don't get to be the manager of Cowdenbeath without knowing how to sign right tits..."

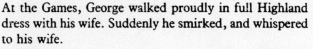

At the Games, George walked proudly in full Highland dress with his wife. Suddenly he smirked, and whispered to his wife.

"What do you think those English tourists would say if I lifted my kilt and flashed my haggis at them, eh?"

His wife grinned.

"They'd say I must have married you for your money."

A wealthy Aberdeen businessman, who regularly played at St Andrews, was taking his secretary away for the weekend. She was a dumb blonde from Carlisle who'd never sampled the high life before.

"So what kind of car is this then?" she asked as he opened the door of his huge limousine.

"It's a Rolls Royce Silver Wraith," the businessman replied proudly.

"Oooh," she said, much impressed. "Are these seats made of real leather?"

"They certainly are. Only the finest Scottish hide..."

"And what does that button do?"

"That controls the in-car entertainment – tape, radio, CD and video in the back."

"And this one?"

"Automatic temperature control. Adjusts the heating and air conditioning to create the perfect conditions whatever the weather's like outside."

Then she spotted three golf tees resting on the dashboard.

"And what are these for?" she enquired.

"Oh those. They're to rest my balls on when I'm driving."

"Ooooh!" she said. "Rolls Royce think of everything!"

A man rushed into the toilet of a pub in Inverness, pulled out an enormous plonker and began peeing liberally.

"Phew!" he gasped. "I only just made it."

A timid man standing next to him looked at his member with awe.

"In that case," he said quietly, "could you make me one?"

Graffiti spotted in a pub in Glasgow:
'Why a man should want to marry a woman is a mystery. Why he should want to marry two women is a bigamistery.'

At a Hogmanay party, a drunken woman stuck her hand up a man's kilt and copped a handful of best Aberdeen Angus.

"Oooh!" she gasped greatly impressed. "What are these for?"

The Scotsman looked puzzled.

"Four?" he said.

A thrifty old man called McEwen
Told people, "Why bother with screwin'?
It's safer and neater
To play with your peter
And besides you can see what you're doin'."

A Scotsman wanted to get married in full Highland dress but so as not to embarrass his shy bride he decided to go against tradition and wear something under his kilt. So the week before his wedding he bought four yards of Stewart tartan and had a pair of matching underpants made. The day after they were ready.

"Here are your undies, Jock," said the tailor. "Mind you, you flatter yourself. I only needed half a yard of your tartan. You can have the rest back."

However, come the day of the wedding, the Scotsman was so nervous he forgot to put his new underpants on, and didn't even notice. Fortunately, neither did the congregation. In fact, all went well. After the ceremony and celebrations, the couple eventually arrived at their honeymoon hotel room.

"Jock, you look really bonnie in your kilt," said his new bride.

"Thank you, my darling, but take a look at this." he replied.

Then full of exuberance and whisky, Jock proudly lifted his kilt to show his wife his hand-made underwear, forgetting once again he had neglected to put it on.

"Pretty good, eh?" he asked proudly.

The shy bride was shocked at the awesome spectacle of his monarch of the glen, and clamped her hand to her mouth. Then a wry smile came to her face.

"Och, Jock, it's lovely," she cooed.

"And that's nothing," replied the Scotsman proudly. "Back at home, there's another three and a half yards you can play with..."

How can you spot a McDonald in the Highlands?
Lift up his kilt. Only McDonalds have quarter-pounders to take out with a big shake.

Big Will McTavish decided to spend his summer holiday in Cuba, but after only a couple of days was desperate for his national drink. So he went into a small bar to order a whisky. Standing beside him were three huge Cubans with bushy beards smoking Havana cigars. Big Will watched jealously as they drank bottle after bottle of the finest whisky and refused to pay. Eventually he just had to ask them their secret.

"We never pay!" boomed one of the three. "We're

Castro's men."

"Oh, I see," said Big Will, and summoned the barman.

"Ten bottles of your finest whisky," he demanded.

The barman fetched it along with an enormous bill.

"I don't pay," boomed Will. "I'm one of Castro's men."

The barman eyed Will's clean-shaven face suspiciously.

"Impossible!" he replied. "All Castro's men have bushy beards and smoke Havana cigars."

Big Will lifted his kilt.

"I'm in the secret service!"

Henry had worked in the Aberdeen branch of the DHSS for 20 years and finally married his childhood sweetheart. However, even on his wedding night, he was keen to apply his organisational brain to their relationship.

"I've been thinking, my dear," he said. "We ought to have some sort of code to let each other know if we fancy making love."

"Och Henry, you're so clever," said his wee wife, "You think of everything."

Henry smiled modestly.

"How about if I want to make love, I kiss you on the left nipple? And if I don't I kiss you on the left nipple again?"

"That's very clever," said his wife. "But what if I want to make love, darling?"

"You pull my wee dangler once," he replied.

"And if I don't?"

"You pull it again," he said. "And again and again and again and..."

WALES

Wales – land of my fathers, or at least most of the suspects. I was born here 33 years ago, the product of love between a man and a woman, and lousy television reception. We lived in a small house on Anglesey – so small the mice were re-accommodated by the council. For my first birthday my parents gave me a carpet. They said I could have it so long as I kept it in the lounge.

These days Wales is a teeming hive of activity. Then on Sunday night, everyone gets in their Volvos and goes back to the South East again. Holiday homes! Yuppies are turning the place into a giant theme park. They're thinking of putting turnstiles up between the Brecon Beacons, and converting Bridgend into a crèche.

Welsh humour is dry (which is more than can be said for the weather) and nicely underplayed. I love it when Welshmen tell jokes. It stops them singing for a few minutes.

A burly Welsh miner and his girl got married and couldn't afford a house of their own or even a honeymoon. Instead they were forced to stay with the girl's mother in a small cottage near Merthyr Tydfil.

The first night after the wedding, the couple were anxious to be alone together, but instead, to be polite, sat with old Mrs Llewellen as she knitted and watched television. However, at ten o' clock, impatience got the better of them. Megan whispered something to her new husband, and then stood up, yawning theatrically.

"Oh well, Mam, it's been a long day. I think I'll be getting to bed now."

"There's a good idea, Megan. Good night, my darling,

sleep well. We'll have a nice walk in the morning..."
replied her mother, barely looking up from her knitting.

After a discreet interval of exactly five minutes filled
with frustrated leg crossing, Dai stood up.

"Ah, er, well now, thanks for everything, Mrs
Llewellen, but I think I'll get some sleep as well now."

"That's right, Dai bach," replied his mother-in-law
quietly. "Now if you want anything..."

Dai never heard the end of the sentence. He was
upstairs, steaming with excitement. He knew his gorgeous
young wife would be waiting for him naked in bed. He
burst into the bedroom.

"Megan, my love," he shouted. "I want to-"

He stopped in his tracks. Instead of lying in bed, Megan
was at the dressing table. Instead of being naked, she was
still wearing her going away dress. Instead of being
deliriously happy, she was in tears.

"Whatever's the matter, my love?" asked Dai.

"Oh, darling, it's the zip on my dress, it's stuck," she
replied.

"Oh Megan, don't worry about that. Look, I've worked
down the pits shifting coal for ten years. I think I can get a
little zip to move a few inches, don't you?"

Megan smiled weakly.

"Oh I do love you, Dai."

However, Dai's confidence was misplaced. Despite his
muscular arms, brawny chest and strong hands, the zip
wouldn't budge. He tried again. Still nothing happened.
Red-faced and sweating with exertion and frustration, he
stripped off his shirt and tried a third time. Still the
fine-toothed barrier between himself and sexual satisfac-
tion remained closed to him. Furious, he stomped towards
the bedroom door.

"Oh, where are you going, Dai?"

"It's no good," he stormed. "I can't get my fingers in

properly. I'll have to cut it."

Down in the small sitting room, Mrs Llewellen could hear thumping and shouting, but carried on with her knitting until Dai burst in semi-naked, red faced and panting.

"Whatever's wrong, Dai?" she asked quietly.

"Mrs Llewellen, I need to borrow your scissors. I must cut a hole in something."

Mrs Llewellen smiled sweetly.

"Oh don't be ridiculous, Dai," she said. "That's the trouble with you miners, you're too heavy-handed. Just tickle it gently, man, and she'll open like a flower."

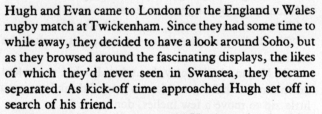

Hugh and Evan came to London for the England v Wales rugby match at Twickenham. Since they had some time to while away, they decided to have a look around Soho, but as they browsed around the fascinating displays, the likes of which they'd never seen in Swansea, they became separated. As kick-off time approached Hugh set off in search of his friend.

After a while a call-girl tapped Hugh on the shoulder, and smiled at him.

"Are you looking for something, love?" she asked wiggling her tightly skirted hips provocatively.

"That's kind of you, dear. Yes, I am as a matter of fact," said Hugh. "I'm looking for Evan."

"You've come to the right place," purred the prostitute. "Follow me."

Hugh happily went with the girl who took him to her flat above a seedy book shop. As they went in, the call-girl lay on the bed and pouted at Hugh, patting the mattress beside her.

"I don't see any sign of Evan here," said the lad from the valleys rather disappointed.

The girl lifted her skirt and opened her legs to reveal she was wearing no knickers.

"There's heaven for you," she whispered.

"Oh no, you're wrong there," replied Hugh disgruntledly. "Evan is a much bigger twat than that..."

Graffiti spotted in a Llangollen pub at Eisteddfod time.

"Marriage is like playing a Stradivarius. Beautiful music with strings attached."

A Welsh sheep farmer was having a driving lesson.

"Now Mr Evans," said the instructor, "can you make a U-turn?"

"No," replied the farmer. "But I could make its eyes water."

Old man Hughes had reached the age of 90 but lost none of his virility. In fact he had just arranged a date with an 18-year-old girl. However, he felt a trip to the doctor's might be a good idea.

"Look, doc, you might find this hard to believe but I've just managed to arrange a date tonight with young Miss Rees from the wool shop," he told him. "Well, she's only a scrap of a thing, and frankly I'm not sure I'm up to it like I was. Is there anything you can give me to help my sex drive?"

"Of course, at your age you need a little assistance," said the GP. "Here take these pills. They're terrific. They'll perk you up no end."

"Thanks, doc,"

The next day Hughes was at the doctor's surgery again this time looking worn out.

"Sorry to trouble you again, doc," he said, "but can I have some pain killers?"

"Certainly!" said the doctor with a chuckle. "For your back no doubt. I said those tablets were good."

"No, actually they're for my wrist," replied Hughes morosely. "She didn't turn up."

A young man deafened in a pit accident sat in a pub in Merthyr watching the barmaid bending down in her skintight jeans as she chatted up the customers.

"Oh, James bach," said his friend. "You must be fed up. You can't hear the way she flirts with you all the time."

"Doesn't matter," he replied. "With jeans that tight, I can read her lips."

A young harlot from near Ebbw Vale
Held cheap nights for the old and frail.
She was easy to find,
And for the aid of the blind,
On her tits were the prices in braille.

Myfanwy had lived in a small cottage in Mid-Wales all her life, and compensated for bouts of loneliness with sudden sessions of wild man-eating. Bored one evening, she decided to dress up and go into town to see if she could find a man for the night. After a few drinks in a club she saw one she fancied and wandered over to him.

"Hi there," she said. "Would you like to come back to my cottage and make love to me all night?"

"Oooh yes, that sounds fun," said the young man, who was also prone to long unrestrained sex sessions.

So they got a taxi back to Myfanwy's cottage. As soon as they got in, Myfanwy pulled her strapless dress down a bit further to reveal bigger mountains than Snowdonia, and fetched her new lover a large brandy. Nervously, the young man looked around. Suddenly he gulped, for there on one wall was a collection of human heads.

"Er excuse me," he asked timidly. "Who are they?"

With a flourish of satin, Myfanwy enfolded him in her arms.

"Why, those are the heads of men who had less than five inches to give me."

The young man swallowed even harder. He knew that size was a problem of his. When last measured he could only muster 3 inches and that was in far less intimidating surroundings.

"But don't let that bother you," continued Myfanwy, kissing him with the force of an industrial vacuum cleaner. "I know you won't let me down. Come into the bedroom – and make me!"

The small-sized man felt smaller still as he was dragged into the bedroom and his head pushed into the valley between her enormous breasts.

"I want you now!" she bellowed.

"Er hang on," he replied, leaping up.

"Where are you going?"

"To the bathroom," he lied, running straight into the kitchen to search for something that might deputise for his insignificant parts. Happily there was a cucumber on the kitchen table, fully ten inches long and an inch and a half across – just what he needed. When he got back to the dark bedroom, he slid beside Myfanwy and started to run the cucumber up her thighs. She giggled excitedly. Then as he reached the top, he pushed the cucumber as far as it would go.

"Oooooooh, oooooh, that's fabulous," cried Myfanwy. "I've always wanted a man who uses his fingers first."

What do fat girls from Bridgend and mopeds have in common?
They're both fun to ride until somebody spots you.

A coachload of Brummies were down in Tenby for the day, and after a few drinks, one of them fell asleep on the beach. For a joke his mates decided to bury him in the sand with just his John Thomas sticking out like a cactus. A little while later, two old ladies who lived in the town were taking their daily constitutional along the front when one spotted the lone tool.

"Now, isn't that just typical?" she sighed. "When I was 10, I knew nothing about them. When I was 20, I was fascinated by them. When I was 30, I couldn't get enough of them. When I was 40, I had to beg for them. When I was 50, I had to pay for them. When I was 60, I could only pray for them. Then finally at 70, I managed to forget about them. Now would you believe it? Tomorrow I'm 80, and the blessed things are growing out the ground."

The residents of the small Welsh fishing village had never been very keen on tourists. They'd watched all the best houses turned into holiday flats, and the smaller ones into *bijou* homes for wealthy Englishmen. In the pub, the attitude was particularly resentful, as Londoners would come in and shout about how quaint the area was. To make matters worse, the local girls were impressed by their money, and tended to go out with them rather than the local lads.

One particularly unpopular man was Cardew Fitzherbert. Every weekend, he'd roar up from Surrey in his sports car, breeze into the pub, and take his pick of any girl he took a fancy to. Then one night, it didn't work. Cardew pushed his way to the bar as usual, downed three gin and tonics and waited for the girls to gather, but they wouldn't. Instead, they sat around a small unimpressive Welshman in the corner, giggling at everything he said.

"I say, girlies," shouted Cardew. "Can I buy any of you sweet things a drink?"

The girls ignored him, and went on canoodling with the shabby Welshman, kissing him and rubbing his chest.

"Look, I've got the Merc outside," he continued. "Fancy a spin at the ton, what?"

Again the girls ignored him, and carried on flirting with the little old man.

Cardew was getting annoyed – nothing seemed to get the local girls away from the physical wreck in the corner. Finally he turned to the barman.

"I say, my good man, who is that old buffer in the corner? Why haven't I seen him before?"

"That's old Meredith," replied the barman. "You wouldn't know him. He normally comes in during the week. He's got a few sheep down the valley."

"Is that all? So why do all the girls go for him?" asked Cardew. "I mean it can't be his looks. You tell me he's just a small-holder so it's not money. What's his chat-up line like?"

"Oh, he doesn't have one," said the barman casually. "Very quiet is Meredith. Generally he just sits in the corner there, licking his eyebrows."

On a day trip to Wales' Colwyn Bay,
Jill boasted to her best friend, Kaye,
"My new boyfriend, Clyde,
Is just like the tide –
In and out at least twice a day."

A little old spinster from Llanelli reached her 100th birthday, and was immediately approached by the local paper who wanted an interview. She agreed and shortly an eager young reporter turned up at her door.

"Now tell me, Mrs Evans, have you managed to keep fit all this time?" he asked.

"I certainly have. In fact I'll have you know I've never seen a doctor in my life."

"Really?" replied the reporter. "Are you saying that in 100 years you've never been bed-ridden once, not even for a short time?"

"No I'm not," she said vehemently. "And I've been had up against the kitchen table as well, but I'm not having you putting that in your paper, boyo."

A Llanferis man Eric Price,
Dabbled in every possible vice.
He had virgins and boys,
And mechanical toys,
And for condoms he used old white mice.

It was a cold winter's day in Pwllheli and Lloyd and his wife were sitting by the fire watching television. After a time, the Welsh documentary proved a little dull for Lloyd, and out of boredom he started wolfing down a bowl of peanuts his wife had put out. When even that failed to inspire him, he started throwing them in the air and trying to catch them in his mouth. As the cold wet evening progressed, Lloyd was getting quite adept at peanut flicking and catching, and was about to attempt a particularly tricky shot, bouncing the peanut off the coffee table, the standard lamp and then into his mouth. Unfortunately, due to a ricochet off the cat, the peanut wedged itself in his ear.

He tried to pick it out with his fingers but to no avail, so eventually he had to wake his wife who had also grown bored with the Welsh documentary.

"Glynis," he said. "I've got a peanut wedged in my ear!"

"Oh, Lloyd, you are stupid. Let me look."

His wife looked in his ear and tried poking about with a knitting needle but only succeeded in pushing the nut further in.

"I've got an idea," she said eventually. "Our Iris has her new boyfriend with her upstairs. He's studying something medical at Bangor University, perhaps he can help."

So Lloyd went upstairs, and knocked on the door. After a few minutes of frantic scrabbling, the student opened it hitching his trousers. Lloyd explained about the peanut, and the eager student said he knew just the cure.

"Now what you do is this," he said. "I'll put two fingers up your nose, and when I tell you to blow, blow as hard as you can."

Lloyd did as he was told and sure enough the peanut flew from his ear.

"Thank you so much," he said and went back down to his wife.

"Well, was Iris's boyfriend able to help?" she asked.

"Yes, he was."

"I told you. There's clever for you. I wonder what he'll become when he leaves university," she mused.

"Well," said her husband, "judging by the smell of his fingers, I'd say our son-in-law."

After falling from a cliff face in Snowdonia, young rock climber Ewan Jones discovered that he could no longer get his parts to stand up and take a bow in the way he would like, so he went to see his GP.

"I'm sorry, Mr Jones, but you've severed all the muscles down there and there's nothing I can do medically."

"That's terrible," cried Ewan. "I'm only 23, and my

wife and I are very active in bed. Isn't there anything I can do?"

"Well, there is this..."

The doctor opened the desk drawer and pulled out a small electronic gadget.

"It's the latest thing from America but it's only on test. In fact, it's the only one ever made."

"What is it?"

"It works on sound waves and triggers muscles in the body which wouldn't ordinarily work. Trouble is, the batteries are very limited."

"So you mean if I wear it, I could get hard again?" asked Ewan excitedly.

"Indeed, but the battery will only power it sufficiently for three goes, and as I said, this is the only one in the world."

"So I have three hard-ons – and that's it? That's better than nothing. How does it work?"

"By sound. You make a high-pitched 'woooo' noise to start it, and a low 'sssshhhh' to stop it," said the doctor.

"I'll give it a go!" said Ewan, had the device fitted and made his way home in the car.

As he stopped at the traffic lights, he thought he'd better test the device, knowing that if it worked, he'd still have two more to enjoy. So he let out a loud 'woooo' and sure enough felt stirrings in his trousers.

"That's fantastic!" he thought, and then went "sssshhhh" to himself to let things drop again. That worked just as well so he hurried home.

Unfortunately he had to stop at the level crossing half a mile from his house to let a train through. Impatiently he tapped the wheel, then the locomotive thundered through. "Woooo" went the whistle, and to Ewan's consternation, his part leaped up again. "Sssshhhh" went the train as it stopped in the station, and his part subsided once more.

"Damn!" he shouted. "That means I've only got one erection left now. I'd better not waste this one."

So that night, he waited as patiently as he could for his wife to put the children to bed, then cuddled up to her by the fire.

"How did you get on at the doctor's, dear?" asked his wife.

"I'm glad you asked me that," he said. "Look at this!"

And with that Ewan stood up and dropped his trousers and pants.

"Woooooooo!" he shouted proudly and his member leaped up bigger and better than ever.

"Sssshhhh!" said his wife, "you'll wake the children."

Two middle-aged men from Cardiff were rugger fanatics, watching every match at the Arms Park. Then one Saturday afternoon, at a particularly crucial moment, one keeled over with a heart attack and died. His friend was distraught. Some weeks after the funeral he still missed his life-long friend. So he decided to visit a spiritualist, and contact his mate on the other side.

When he got there, the spiritualist made him sit down at a table with a cloth, and then started chanting. Suddenly, he heard his friend's voice.

"Owen, is that you?" he asked.

"Hello, Hugh lad," said the voice.

"What's it like in heaven? You are in heaven, aren't you?"

"I'm in heaven, Hugh, and it's wonderful. They have sweet music, lovely food and decent beer. It's beautiful."

"But do they have rugby, Owen?"

"Oh, they have rugby all right. In fact, I've got the team list with me. I'm playing prop forward on Saturday."

"That's fantastic, Hugh."

Suddenly it went quiet.

"Oh dear," said the voice from beyond.

"What's up, Hugh?"

"It's the team list, man."

"What's the problem?"

"Well, I don't know how to put this but in a fortnight's time you're down to play scrum half."

A young man from Anglesey went to his local doctor following some tests for his illness and was given some bad news.

"I'm sorry, Mr Jones, but I'm afraid the results of the tests show that you only have six months to live."

"Oh God!" he cried. "Whatever am I going to do?"

"If I were you, I'd go to Bridgend, find a fat noisy woman, marry her and start watching English soccer on television."

"Will that help, doctor?"

"In a way. It'll make six months seem like a lifetime."

Overheard in a pub in Cardiff.

"My Megan is so frigid, every time she opens her legs, the central heating comes on."

NORTHERN
IRELAND

Sadly I've never been to Northern Ireland myself, but I have several friends from that part of Britain. Take Anna, for example. She's from Londonderry and has an accent that could slice bricks. She only has one vowel sound – 'Arrr'. As a voice test for the BBC, they asked her to read a nursery rhyme. 'Marrry harrrd arrr larrrtle larrrm...' she began. They stopped her before the windows broke.

Of course, there's only one story that ever comes out of Northern Ireland, and that's 'the troubles'. I know all there is to know about that. I've had them myself after ten pints of draught Guinness. Believe me, it gives 'conflict on the Bog Side', a whole new meaning.

Like lots of areas with problems, out of turmoil humour blossoms. I must go there this year...

A Ballycastle man was referred to the psychiatrist because he was fixated with women's breasts. Every day he'd sit on a bench watching boobs bouncing by, and in the pub he would stare down the cleavage of the barmaid. Even his wife found that he wouldn't make love to her any more. All he wanted to do was cuddle her enormous bosoms, so she made an appointment for him with the shrink.

"Now then, Mr Casey," said the doctor. "I understand your problem is breasts. Perhaps we could start with a simple word association test to judge the extent of the problem, could we?"

"Whatever you say, doc," he replied meekly.

"Right then, I'll give you a word and you tell me the first thing that comes into you head. Okay, Mr Casey?"

"Fine."

"Right," said the psychiatrist. "Melons."

"Breasts," said Mr Casey.

"Coconuts."

"Breasts."

"Headlamps."

"Breasts."

"Windscreen wipers."

"Breasts," smiled the old man.

"Now hold on," said the shrink. "I don't understand. Melons, coconuts, even headlamps, yes, but what on earth have windscreen wipers got to do with a woman's boobs?"

"It's obvious," replied the old man, and his head started bobbing from side to side. "Kiss this one, then that one. Kiss this one, then that one..."

A Belfast off-licence owner was just closing for the night when a nun came through the door. The proprietor looked a little surprised, then asked what the Sister wanted.

"I'd like a bottle of brandy," said the nun.

"But we don't normally serve nuns with strong drink," he replied.

"Oh I know," said the nun, "but it's for medical reasons. Mother Superior is suffering from terrible constipation."

"Oh I see," said the owner. "All right then."

The nun left the store with the brandy and the owner carried on locking up. By the time he'd finished and done his books, it was getting late. Then, as he made his way home, he saw a black mound in the middle of the pavement. It was dark and he couldn't work out what it was. When he got nearer, however, he could see it was the nun slumped over the now three-quarters empty brandy bottle.

"Hello there," she slurred waving the bottle at him. "Thanksshh for the drinksshh."

The off-licence proprietor was furious.

"What do you mean by this?" he demanded. "I only agreed to sell you that alcohol because you assured me it was to cure your Mother Superior's constipation."

"Oh it isshh," replied the nun. "When she sees me she'll fill her knickers!"

Two leprechauns knocked on the door of a convent in County Antrim. The Mother Superior answered.

"Well, if it's not the little people," she said. "Now what can I be doing for you?"

"Hello there," said one of the leprechauns. "My friend here was just wondering if you'd have such a thing as a leprechaun nun."

The Mother Superior laughed.

"A leprechaun nun!" she exclaimed. "I don't think so."

"Thank you," he replied and vanished.

Some minutes later they knocked on the door of another convent. Again the Mother Superior answered the door.

"Excuse me but my friend here was wondering if you have such a thing as a leprechaun nun," said the spokesman for the little people again.

"I'm sorry, but no," replied the Mother Superior.

So the two leprechauns went on their way to a third convent and asked the same question.

"No, I'm afraid not," said the Mother Superior. "There's no such thing" and she shut the door.

The leprechaun turned to his mate.

"There I told you it was a penguin you've been shagging!"

How do you make a hormone in Derry?
Put sand in her Vaseline.

There was a young man called O'Neill
Used to play on an old Campanile.
He made the gong bong,
With the aid of his dong.
Now he's waiting for the poor thing to heal.

There was an old man called O'Malley
Who was bonking young Sal in an alley.
When right at the start,
She let out a loud fart,
Said O'Malley to Sally, 'Oh r'ally!'

A little Irishman was sitting with his friend on the train
after an unsuccessful day at the races. As his mate went to
buy a few more tins of Guinness to help drown their
sorrows, an old lady sharing their compartment leaned
over and patted him on the knee.

"Don't be so miserable," she said. "You're a kind man,
your reward will come in heaven. I couldn't help
overhearing what you were saying and I think putting
your shirt on that poor horse that got scratched was the
most considerate thing I've ever hear ."

After years of sexual failure on the grounds of his minuscule member, Brian was walking through Portrush when a leprechaun appeared.

"Ah Brian," said the little leprechaun. "You've caught me and you can have any wish you like come true."

"Okay," said Brian. "I wish I had a donger that reached to the ground."

"Certainly," said the leprechaun, and chopped his legs off.

In order to encourage the children to learn more rapidly, the teacher at the Donegal school decided to instigate a system of rewards.

"Now what I'm going to do, children, is read you a story from the Bible and then ask a question about it. Whoever gets it right can have the rest of the afternoon off."

The children gasped at the prospect, and most made a special attempt to listen to the story.

On Wednesday, she told the story of Joseph and Jacob, and asked who had the coat of many colours? Mary Malone's hand shot up.

"Joseph, miss."

"Very good, Mary. Have the rest of the afternoon off."

On Thursday she told the story of Lot and asked who was turned into a pillar of salt? Another hand shot up.

"Lot's wife, miss," said Colin Rafferty.

"That's right, Colin," replied the teacher. "Take the rest of the afternoon off."

Now young Brendan had no interest in Bible stories but he had watched the smarter kids getting to go home early, and was beginning to feel jealous. However, he knew he never had any idea what the answers were, so he contented himself with playing with his marbles.

Come Friday, the teacher was reading the story of Esau and Isaac, and Brendan was playing with two particularly fine allies he'd won that very morning. They were black as jet and almost as big as golf balls. The teacher reached the end of the story.

"Now children, it's question time," said the teacher. "Remember, who gets it right has the rest of the afternoon off. Now…"

At that point, Brendan dropped his marbles and they rolled noisily towards the teacher.

"Okay," she said. "Who's the comedian with the two black balls?"

Brendan seized his chance.

"Lenny Henry," he said. "See you Monday."

What's the difference between a Derry wedding and a Derry funeral?
One less drunk.

Mick decided that it was time to impress his girlfriend so he took her for a lavish weekend at the Europa Hotel. They'd had a very comfortable night, and they came down for breakfast feeling positively romantic.

The dining room was crowded with all nationalities, and Mick, who wasn't used to high society, sat dumbfounded by the whole thing. Breakfast was served, and he listened to the conversations that were going on around him, hoping to get a clue as to what to say in these surroundings.

At the next table there was a French couple, obviously deeply in love, and enjoying the atmosphere. Mick listened to their conversation, then heard the Frenchman asked for the sugar.

"Pass me the sugar, sugar," he said.

Mick was most impressed. The girl positively cooed. He must try something like that. Then from the other side, he heard an English couple.

"I say, pass me the honey, honey," said the Englishman.

Again, the girl was over the moon at this romantic way of asking for such a simple thing. There was nothing for it, thought Mick, he'd have to come up with an equally impressive gesture. He thought long and hard, then suddenly inspiration struck. He lent over, smiled and whispered in his love's ear.

"Pass me the bacon, pig."

Two Catholics were sitting in the waiting room of the maternity ward. Both had been pacing for hours when suddenly the nursing sister appeared.

"Mr O'Leary?"

"Yes, Sister?" replied one of the men.

"Congratulations! You've got a seven pound baby boy."

But instead of being happy, the man burst into tears.

"What's the matter?" asked the other expectant father.

"Another boy!" he sobbed. "That makes ten. One more and I've got my own football team!"

"That's nothing," came the reply. "I've got 17 daughters. One more and I've got a golf course."

Why do the kids south of the border make good astronauts?
They take up space in school.

Patrick was playing golf when yet another leprechaun appeared on the course.

"Top of the morning to you," said the little leprechaun. "I'm going to let you have any wish you like, but there's a catch."

"What's the catch?" asked Patrick.

"You're only allowed to have sex once a year."

"Okay," said Patrick. "In that case, I wish I was the greatest golfer in the world."

"Are you sure you don't mind about the sex?" asked the leprechaun.

"Not at all," replied Patrick. "You see, I only have sex six times a year anyway."

"Only six times!" exclaimed the leprechaun. "Why's that?"

"Well, I've only got a small parish."

A nervous young priest asked the Father for advice when he was about to give his first sermon.

"I need something to help me with my nerves," he said.

"Oh that's simple," the Father replied. "Have a couple of Jamiesons before you start. That always works wonders."

So the young priest did as he was advised, though

through youthful enthusiasm had rather more than he should. However, his sermon went down fantastically well and, rather proud of himself, he asked the Father how he thought he'd done.

"Well, you got the congregation on your side which is a start," said the Father, "but I did notice a couple of points."

"Oh what were they?"

"Well, firstly there were 12 disciples not ten, and 10 commandments not 12. Next, David slew Goliath – he did not kick the crap out of him. I'd prefer it if Jesus and the disciples were not called JC and the lads, and the Blessed Virgin is not normally known as Mary with the cherry. Oh and worst of all, please never refer to the crucified body of Christ as Mr T."

The young priest was mortified.

"I'm sorry, Father. I got carried away. In future, I'll just announce the church events like before."

"I'd rather you didn't, son," said the Father. "I'm going to have enough trouble explaining this week's. There is a Tug of War at St Peter's tomorrow – not a Tug of Peter's at St Wars!"

A priest from Derry had been invited over to America for an ecumenical visit. He'd been met at New York by a Rabbi who'd also been invited and together they got on the small local airline to take them to their destination. However, not long into the flight, the plane developed engine trouble. It started to plummet from the skies, and the passengers began to scream.

Immediately the priest knelt down in the aisle, crossed himself and started praying. Then he looked up and noticed to his surprise that the Rabbi was also crossing himself. At last the pilot regained control of the aircraft and the plane began to level out, and with great relief the priest sat down again next to the Rabbi.

"I see that at a time when you fear death even you Rabbis turn to the Almighty Jesus for help," he commented with a smile.

"Not at all, not at all," replied the Rabbi.

"But I saw you crossing yourself," the priest said.

"Cross myself? Certainly not, just the traditional Jewish check at times like these – spectacles, testicles, money and cigars!"

Did you hear what happened when Paddy O'Reilly was told that he had sugar in his urine? He started pissing on his corn flakes.

Sean O'Casey started work as a surgeon last week. His first job was a circumcision. Unfortunately he missed and got the sack.

Seamus was an all-time loser. Suffering from acne from the age of 11 to adulthood, he was ignored by girls all his life. So he decided to become a flasher. However, on his very first attempt, he was caught and charged with indecent exposure. As if that wasn't bad enough, the hearing was held in the small claims court.

The Northern Ireland Tourist Board has just announced that it intends to abandon a new brochure promoting activities on the east coast on Saturdays and Sundays. The leaflet was to be called "Why Not Bangor this Weekend?"

A naughty young girl called O'Dare
Sailed on a ship to Rosslaire,
But this cute little honey
Had forgotten her money,
So she was laid by the crew for her fare.

Dermot decided to blow his money on a month-long holiday at a nudist camp. His mother was a puritanical soul, and wouldn't have approved, so he told her he was going to Butlins. However, after three weeks he realised he would have to send her a postcard.

The only postcards available showed nude people cavorting around the place, so he decided to send his best wishes on a photograph of himself at the camp. That too was nude, but if he cut the bottom half off it, it would at least show how tanned and healthy he was now. So he did just that, but unfortunately in his hurry to catch the post, he sent the wrong half of his photo.

Within two days, his mother had written back.

"Thank you for the card," she said. "You're right. You are nice and brown, but that new hairstyle of yours is terrible. It makes you look really old and your nose too long!"

Three nuns were confessing their sins to their Mother Superior.

"Oh, Holy Mother," said the first, "Last night I went into town with these two other girls and I saw a man's private parts."

"Bless you, my child," replied the Mother Superior. "Now go and wash your face in Holy Water."

The second nun looked even more apologetic.

"Oh Holy Mother," she said. "When I went to town with the two other girls I touched a man's private parts."

"Oh dear God," said the Mother Superior. "Never mind, my child, wash your hands in the Holy Water."

Just as the second nun was about to leave the third nun grabbed hold of her.

"Sister Theresa," she whispered, "when you wash your hands, don't go making the Holy Water too messy, will you? I'm going to have to gargle in that in a minute."

A 90-year-old Fermanagh man went to a sperm bank offering to make a donation. The nurse tried to keep a straight face.

"You know how the sperm bank works, don't you?" she said with a giggle in her voice. "It's for donations not withdrawals."

"I know that," said the proud old man. "I've come to make a deposit."

"Well, if you're sure you're up to it," said the nurse. "I'll get you a jar, and you can go behind that screen over there."

She brought the jar and the old man took it behind the screen. For some time all that could be heard was terrible grunting, then panting and shouting. All the nurses gathered round whispering to themselves when they heard what was going on. Finally there was a thumping sound, and the old man emerged red-faced and bathed in sweat, with the jar still empty.

"Didn't you manage, sir?" asked the nurse politely.

The old man scowled.

"I tried it with the left hand," he said. "I tried it with the right. I've pushed it and pulled it. I've even bashed it against the wall a few times. But I'm damned if I can get the top off this jar of yours."

Father Docherty had been training his young curate for some years, then one day told him that it was time for him to hear his first confession.

"But how will I know what to give as penances?" he asked.

"That's simple," the priest replied. "There's a list on your side of the confessional box."

"Okay, Father," he said and went to the church.

He sat down and immediately a voice came through the grille.

"Forgive me," it said, "but last night I took strong drink."

The curate consulted his list.

"Say three Hail Marys," he replied and the parishioner went away.

"Forgive me," came a second voice shortly after, "but last night I committed adultery."

The curate looked at the list again.

"Say five Hail Marys," he replied and again the parishioner left satisfied.

This happened several times and the curate was feeling quite proud of the way he was handling things when suddenly a girl's voice came through the grille.

"Forgive me," she said. "But last night I had oral sex."

The curate examined the list. There was no mention of oral sex. He panicked and rushed out of the box. He didn't know what to do, then he spotted an angelic choirboy entering the stalls before practice that afternoon.

"Can you help me?" the curate asked. "Do you know what Father Docherty gives for oral sex?"

"Well it depends," said the sweet innocent child. "But generally I get a bottle of pop and a packet of crisps."

Two post office counter clerks in Belfast became obsessed with the size of their female colleague's boobs. For hours they'd watch as they swayed in her jumper, and often they'd drop things, just so they could watch her bend down and pick them up.

"They're fantastic," said one. "They must be 42 inches at least."

"Imagine holding them," said his friend. "How much do you think they weigh?"

"There's an easy way to find out. Next time she bends over the parcels scale, I'll unclip her bra, and when they fall on to the scales, you read off the weight."

"That's a good idea."

So next time she was in the right vicinity, the first clerk turned to her.

"Now, Mary could I be borrowing some first class stamps, please?" he asked seemingly innocently.

"Why sure, Michael," she replied and leaned over the parcels scale to reach the book. As soon as she did Michael reached up her jumper, unclipped her bra and with a heavy plop-plop, her boobs fell on to the weighing surface.

When she realised what had happened, she screamed and ran into the back room.

Michael turned to his accomplice.

"Now tell me did you see how much they weighed?" he asked.

"Not exactly," he replied. "But I can tell you they'd cost £2.30 to send anywhere in Europe."

There was a young man called Sean
Who wished he'd never been born.
And he wouldn't have been,
If his father had seen
That the end of his condom was torn.

A farmer we know called O'Doole
Had a long and incredible tool,
He could use it to plough,
Or pleasure a cow,
Or just as a cue-stick at pool.